A Marvelous World

❧ A MARVELOUS WORLD
POEMS BY BENJAMIN PÉRET

Translated, with an Introduction,
by Elizabeth R. Jackson

A bilingual edition

LOUISIANA STATE UNIVERSITY PRESS
BATON ROUGE AND LONDON

The original French poems in this volume are taken from Benjamin
Péret, *Oeuvres complètes*, copyright © Editions Eric Losfeld-Le Terrain Vague,
Paris, 1969–1971.

Translations, Introduction, Chronology, and Appendix
copyright © 1985 by Elizabeth R. Jackson
Manufactured in the United States of America

Design: Albert Crochet
Typeface: Linotron Galliard
Composition: G&S Typesetters, Inc.
Printing and Binding: Edwards Brothers, Inc.

LIBRARY OF CONGRESS CATALOGING IN PUBLICATION DATA

Péret, Benjamin.
   A marvelous world.

   I. Title.
PQ2631.E348A24   841'.912   80-13631
ISBN 0-8071-0664-X

*To the memory of Herbert and
Inge Marcuse, kindred spirits*

Contenu

vi

Contents

Acknowledgments

In the preparation of this work, many people have contributed their assistance and supportive spirit. Eric Losfeld, known for his editions, "Le Terrain vague," long ago recognized Benjamin Péret's true worth. He was helpful to me for many years in my work—through his publications presenting the vital depth of Péret and by making available materials for this volume. Following his untimely death, his wife Pierrette Losfeld along with L'Association des amis de Benjamin Péret have furthered these efforts. The source of the French versions of the poems in this book is his two-volume edition of Benjamin Péret's *Oeuvres complètes* (Paris: Le Terrain Vague, 1969–71). François Chapon, curator of the collection of the Bibliothèque Doucet, which includes a number of Péret's manuscripts and many of the original editions of his publications, has been most helpful and obliging. As for the preparation of the typescript of the present volume, I am indebted to Madeleine Strauss, especially to her sense of the force of the "word on the page." For the preparation of the translations, I consider myself fortunate to have had the editorial assistance of Patricia Cope, whose judgment is so finely tuned to the "word in depth" of this humanely critical Surrealist poet. My sincere thanks to all.

Introduction

"Birds fly, fish swim, and men invent," says Benjamin Péret. His poetic world is literally a marvelous invention, so much so that, on entering it, one must first expect the unexpected and then be prepared to enjoy the game as it is proposed or to share in the horrors and ecstasies of extraordinary dramatic situations. Suspension of disbelief is, in this case, an absolute necessity.

Péret is a Surrealist's Surrealist. A member of the movement from its beginning—although unembroiled in its major controversies on a personal level—especially and naturally dedicated to writing poetry that would embody the "fonctionnement réel de l'esprit"—the basic goal of Surrealism— he was and is appreciated fully by those closest to the core of the movement but as yet has not received his due share of serious attention from critics and is relatively unknown to the general public. This volume includes poems from all his major poetic works, selected for their excellence and for their variety of tone and focus. These poems represent a view of his world, a world that will reveal its "marvelous" features while preserving a good measure of mystery and puzzlement. Broader appreciation of the poems and of the world they represent will, I hope, allow their creator to emerge from the ranks of unknown artists to join others whose creations also exhibit imaginative structures disturbingly different from what we are accustomed to in day-to-day life. Paul Klee, Joan Miró, and Lewis Carroll come to mind as fellow artistic spirits.

As a political revolutionary, Péret actively attacked existing systems and ideologies. As a Surrealist, he contested rationalism—the view of man as essentially rational and the view that reason is the best or the only source of knowledge. However, the main import of his ideas about poetry and the poetry itself is positive in aim and effect. As suggested by the initial quotation, invention, imaginative thought, and creation define the basic activity of human beings, define their unique features, define what they do most and what they do best. Péret was particularly interested in the primitive mentality. Having lived in South America and Mexico, he studied popular cultures, their art, myths, legends, and the Mayan religion. In various essays, he speaks of prerational thought as a more direct and effective means of contacting the world, reflecting the world, and understanding the world. The contact is more direct; the original unity between man and the universe is preserved; and an affectivity—an energy—is engendered that can reinforce natural bonds between an individual and the world and within the community of human beings.

This type of consciousness is poetic. In one essay, Péret mentions particular feelings, such as overwhelming sadness at the sight of snow, flake by flake smothering all sounds, or the enchantment evoked by a lily of the valley. Generalizing, he points out certain archetypal images, such as the serpent, which have a universal psychic significance; and he emphasizes the timelessness of such basic emotions as fright, anguish, melancholy, and enchantment. All of these perceptions constitute what Péret means by the *marvelous*—a key word for him, as it is for other Surrealists. Especially important for an understanding of his poetry is the fact that, for him, the marvelous can be found anywhere. All that is necessary is to remain open to possibilities, to be interested in what may be disclosed. "It's there," he says, "hidden from ordinary people but ready to explode like a time bomb. This drawer I open shows me an absinthe spoon amongst spools of thread and compasses. Through the holes in the spoon a band of tulips doing the goose-step come to meet me." And thus the adventure begins. Perhaps the most important clue to be gained from this explanation is that his poetic world is not by any means totally divorced from what we commonly call reality, but is instead an extension of the real world. That is what "surrealism" is, in fact. The starting point is our own experience—reactions, emotions, creatures, things, situations—and the world that it leads to continues to exhibit some familiar features, including some sort of structure. For Péret's goal was to recapture an original conceptual unity.

Yet one wonders what sort of unity it is and how to deal with its absurd elements. These are problems for the reader and also for the translator. What kind of sense can or should be made of a poem? Certainly some sort of sense, even if it is as simple as a sense of play; otherwise, there would be no reason for the poem's existence and no appeal. However, the communication is nondiscursive, since the aim above all is to avoid the traditional view of poetry as a form of expression involving ideas and personal feelings.

As a translator, the unity I have sought is a unity of focus. There are many varieties: word games, tonal sketches, a political event eliciting ridicule and outrage, pure adventure, human relationships (as in the love poems), unearthly scenarios fraught with deep-lying anguish, humor based on incongruous but recognizable combinations of characters and attributes. In each poem, when in doubt regarding a choice of English equivalents, I have looked for a word that would be consistent with the given focus. For instance, the range of English in "Mexican Air" contains many more poetically dense traditional literary terms and fewer modern idiomatic choices because the overall proportions of the poem are epic. In other poems, I have used truisms and colloquial expressions if the focus is playful and if the original generally contains such terms in French. As for form in a purely mechanical sense, I felt it was essential to respect the length of line and the grammatical coordination. Consistently, Péret ends a line with a complete grammatical expression and begins the next with a qualifying phrase or clause, a causal expression, or even an altogether new proposition. In this respect, his prosody could hardly be more conservative. This division of lines is important for emphasis and for rhythmic effect, and it aids immensely in keeping the narrative straight. As for rhythm and sounds within lines, I have also kept as close as possible to the original, since the tonal impact is closely related to those elements. Péret practiced "automatic writing" quite naturally, composing poems anywhere, on any scrap of paper, with very few revisions. But the few manuscripts available with corrections show that any changes still preserved the original rhythm and stayed close to the original sound patterns.

Perhaps one of the most interesting features of Péret's poetry is his conception of language as evidenced in that poetry. Sometimes Humpty-Dumpty's words are quoted in connection with Surrealist writing: "When I use a word it means exactly what I want it to mean." I do not think this holds true for Péret. His words are used quite carefully, and their meaning does not appear to be subjectively altered. For instance, if he says, "The geranium only dreams about the full moon," he does mean *geranium*, having expressly chosen the geranium to be a character in that part of the story. Causal expressions that occur frequently also retain their meaning. When he says, "But now the world stops being frozen / and the storm with peacock's eyes slides under it / because everything is dark," the cause-and-effect sequence is completely plausible in the context of the given elements, even though some of those elements are strange to us. Péret's intention in most cases is quite clear and intelligible. Consequently, I have not taken any liberties translating conjunctions or nouns (with a few exceptions), simply because there was no need to. Similarly, the tenses of verbs presented no problems and in fact were crucial for maintaining clear temporal relationships within the narrative.

On the other hand, adjectives and verbs, because of the nature of each word itself, sometimes made choices unavoidable. Semantically this is interesting, since frequently it shows how, within these classes of words, an adjective denotes, not essences, but attributes, and a verb cannot be defined uniquely but instead designates a specific action whose verbal description will vary depending on the circumstances (who is doing what, where, and when). An example of such an ordinary adjective is *étonné*, which in English has a considerable range of equivalents, each quite different in nuance—*stunned, surprised, amazed*. An example of such a verb is *jaillir*, which in English can be translated "to spring up," "to shoot forth," "to gush," "to squirt," and so on. To translate the first line of "Mexican Air"—"Le feu vêtu de deuil jaillit par tous ses pores"—I used *spurts* because it is an appropriately strong word, appropriate semantically with *fire*, and with a low degree of impertinence paired with *pores*. So in these instances my choice was to restrain any tendency toward further absurdity.

Curiously, a frequent difficulty involved articles. Péret used the definite article predominantly. Therefore it was necessary to determine as carefully as possible whether, in each case, the definite article signified the general class of the noun, the thing involved—in which case I omitted the article entirely in English—or the particular thing that he was using as a character in the story—in which case I kept the definite article in English. Beyond that, it appeared that sometimes he used the singular definite article where the indefinite article in English sounded more appropriate. Some lines from "Le Quart d'une vie" read like this:

"Vers le ciel de juillet
montent les fourrures ovipares
Le serrurier militaire
invente le contrepoint
nécessaire à la nourriture des abeilles

In my translation, I used "*A* military locksmith," since it figured in a small isolated scene. In such a case, I think Péret may have wished to emphasize that he conceived of each person or object as a special hero or character, giving them the privilege of taking part in a unique drama. The key question is one of specificity. It appears likely that the degree of specificity in the alternate choice between definite article or indefinite article in French is not perfectly equivalent to the similar choice in English. The above example combines a specific occurrence with a nonspecific but limited reference.

One of the most interesting features of Péret's poetry is his use of noun and verb qualifiers. André Breton once asked a provocative question: "Does not the mediocrity of our universe depend upon our power of enunciation?" This concerns one of the prime functions of language, that of naming objects, which involves also giving them some degree of definition, showing how each thing is unique or different. There is an Eskimo dialect that has many separate words to designate different kinds of snow; in that respect, their language—and therefore their world—is richer than ours in that it provides separately focused expressions for a variety of natural phenomena. When Péret creates new characters for his narratives, usually anthropomorphizing inanimate objects, he often describes them carefully by using noun or verb qualifiers connected to the main noun with the prepositions *à* or *de*. Often the combinations are surreal. In so doing, he designates primary rather than secondary attributes. The effect is to people an invented world with beings colorful to us by virtue of exact definitions that combine elements unusual in our experience. One poem is based exactly on this type of word formation and personifying technique. The poem includes the lines:

Petite vaisselle
aboutira
Beurre d'oiseau
grandira
Pelle de sel
patinera
. . .
Cigare de nuage
s'encanaillera
Carte à oreilles
bourgeonnera

Some of these lines are hard to translate because they are hard to envisage. For instance, is "cigare de nuage" a cigar-shaped cloud or a cigar made of clouds? My translation in this case avoided the issue neatly by leaving the same ambiguity in English—"cloud cigar." In any event, the creation is interesting and unforgettable.

I hope that Péret's sense of original unity and universal harmony has been respected in these translations. His *Histoire naturelle*, an account of the creation of the world, contains the following passage: "nothing led to suppose that one day harmony would reign, when the sky appeared to clear and the storm passed over . . . a rainbow sparkled above the fascinated earth. The vegetation understood and, without talking, each plant noiselessly occupied the corner destined for it." If each word in these translations similarly appears noiselessly to occupy the place in the poem destined for it, then the harmony of Péret's world will be sufficiently preserved.

Chronology

1899	Born in Rézé, near Nantes.*
1917–19	Military service. Finds book of Stéphane Mallarmé's poetry on a bench in a railway station.
1920	Meets André Breton, Louis Aragon, Paul Éluard and Philippe Soupault.
1920–22	Participation in Dada movement.
1921	Publication of *Le Passager du transatlantique* (Paris: Collection "Dada").
1923	Publication of *Au 125 du boulevard Saint-Germain* (Paris: Collection "Littérature").
1924	Publication of *Immortelle maladie* (Paris: Collection "Littérature").
1924–25	Coeditor of *La Révolution surréaliste*.
1925	Publication of *Il était une boulangère* (Paris: Aux Éditions du Sagittaire) and of *152 Proverbes mis au goût du jour*, with Paul Éluard (Paris: Éditions surréalistes).
1927	Joins the Communist party and works for a time with *L'Humanité*. Marries Elsie Houston, a Brazilian singer. Publication of *Dormir dormir dans les pierres* (Paris: Éditions surréalistes) and of *Au Grand jour*, with Louis Aragon, André Breton, Paul Éluard, and Pierre Unik (Paris: Éditions surréalistes).
1928	Publication of *. . . Et les Seins mouraient . . .* (Paris: Les Cahiers du Sud) and of *Le Grand jeu* (Paris: Gallimard).
1929–31	Resides in Brazil.

* Biographical information about Benjamin Péret is available in the following works: Jean-Louis Bédouin, *Benjamin Péret* (Paris: Seghers, 1961); Julia Costich, *The Poetry of Change: A Study of the Surrealist Works of Benjamin Péret* (North Carolina Studies in the Romance Languages and Literatures, No. 206) (Chapel Hill: University of North Carolina Press, 1979); Claude Courtot, *Introduction à la lecture de Benjamin Péret* (Paris: Terrain vague, 1965); and J. H. Matthews, *Benjamin Péret* (Boston: Twayne, 1975). Professor Matthews' book was especially helpful in preparing my brief chronology of Péret's life and works.

1929	Publication of *1929*, with Louis Aragon and Man Ray (no publisher).
1931	Birth of his son, Geyser, in Rio de Janeiro. Joins the Communist league of opposition. Imprisoned and expelled from Brazil for political activities.
1931–35	Returns to Paris where he continues political activities.
1934	Publication of *De Derrière les fagots* (Paris: Éditions surréalistes).
1935	Trip to the Canary Islands for the opening of an international Surrealist exhibition.
1936	Publication of *Je ne mange pas de ce pain-là* (Paris: Éditions surréalistes), *Je sublime* (Paris: Éditions surréalistes), and *Trois cerises et une sardine* (Paris: Éditions G.L.M.).
1936–38	With Republican forces in the Spanish Civil War.
1938	Publication of *Au Paradis des fantômes* (Paris: Collection "Un Divertissement").
1940	Recalled to military service (February). Arrested for political activity; imprisoned in Rennes (May). Released, paying ransom to German forces (July). Resides in Paris clandestinely until the end of the year, then joins Surrealist friends in Marseilles.
1940–48	Resides in Mexico.
1942	Publication of *Les Malheurs d'un dollar* (Paris: Éditions de la Main à Plume).
1943	After the death of Elsie Houston, marries Remedios Varo, a painter. Publication of *La Parole est à Péret* (New York: Éditions surréalistes).
1945	Publication of *Le Déshonneur des poètes* (Mexico City: Poésie et Révolution) and of *Dernier malheur dernière chance* (Paris: Éditions de la revue *Fontaine*).
1946	Breaks with the IVth International; publishes *Manifeste des exégètes*, under the pseudonym Peralta. Publication of *Main forte*, collective edition (Paris: Éditions de la revue *Fontaine*).
1947	Publication of *Feu central*, collective edition (Paris: Éditions K).
1948	Returns to Paris; works as a proofreader.
1949	Publication of *La Brebis galante* (Paris: Les Éditions premières).
1952	Publication of *Air mexicain* (Paris: Librairie Arcanes).
1953	Publication of *Mort aux vaches et au champ d'honneur* (Paris: Éditions Arcanes) and of *Toyen*, with André Breton and Jindrich Heisler (Paris: Éditions Sokolova).
1954	Brief trip to Spain. Publication of *Les Rouilles encagées*, published under the pseudonym Satyremont (Paris: Losfeld).

1955	Trip to Brazil to study pre-Columbian and popular art. Publication of *Le Livre de Chilám Balám Chumayel* (Paris: Denoël), translation of a Spanish version of a Mayan religious text.
1956	Publication of *Anthologie de l'amour sublime* (Paris: Éditions Albin Michel).
1957	Publication of *Le Gigot, sa vie et son oeuvre*, collective edition (Paris: Le Terrain vague).
1958	Publication of *Histoire naturelle* (Manosque: Ussel).
1959	Dies in Paris.
1960	Publication of *Anthologie des mythes, légendes et contes populaires d'Amérique* (Paris: Éditions Albin Michel).
1963	Publication of *Dames et généraux* (Milan: Schwarz; Paris: Berggruen).
1965	Publication of *Pour un second Manifeste communiste*, with G. Munis (Paris: Le Terrain vague).
1968	Publication of *Les Mains dans les poches* (Montpellier: Léo Éditeur) and of *Les Syndicats contre la révolution*, with G. Munis (Paris: Le Terrain vague).
1969	Publication of *Oeuvres complètes*, Vol. I (Paris: Losfeld).
1971	Publication of *Oeuvres complètes*, Vol. II (Paris: Losfeld).

A Marvelous World

❦ LE PASSAGER DU TRANSATLANTIQUE

En avant

En avant disait l'arc-en-ciel matinal
En avant pour les soupiraux de notre jeunesse
Nous avons éclaté
et tout ce qui était bleu est resté bleu

En souvenir des petits oignons
que tu mettais dans les chrysanthèmes
dis bonjour à la dame

Avant casse ta tête
ou celle de ton voisin le plus proche
en sorte que tous les deux
nous prendrons l'Orient-Express aux prochaines vacances

Babord pour tous

Babord détachez mon cerveau bleu
Babord éloignez mon voisin de gauche
Babord donnez-moi de l'eau potable
Babord prenez garde aux montagnes
Babord songez à l'arsenic
Babord changez l'encre qui est jaune
Babord protégez-moi des courants d'air
Babord souvenez-vous de l'année dernière
Babord souvenez-vous de la chaleur
Babord souvenez-vous des promeneurs de cactus
car nous passons

❦ THE PASSENGER ON THE TRANSATLANTIC LINER

Full Speed Ahead

Full speed ahead said the early-morning rainbow
Full speed ahead for the vents of our youth
We've exploded
and everything that was blue stayed blue

In remembrance of the little onions
that you put in the chrysanthemums
say hello to the lady

First break your head
or your closest neighbor's
so that both of us
will take the Orient-Express for our next vacation

Port It's for Everybody

Port unlash my blue brain
Port get my neighbor on the left out of the way
Port give me some drinking water
Port look out for the mountains
Port contemplate the arsenic
Port change the yellow ink
Port protect me from drafts
Port remember last year
Port remember the heat
Port remember the cactus walkers
for we're going along

nous passons et les hirondelles passent avec nous
mais nous crachons en l'air
et les hirondelles crachent sur nous

Passagers de seconde classe et leurs cheveux

J'y cours
Où courez-vous
Nulle part
Moi aussi
Alors

we're going along and the swallows are going with us
but we're spitting in the air
and the swallows are spitting on us

Second-Class Passengers and Their Hair

I'm running
Where are you running
Nowhere
So am I
Well

✿ DORMIR DORMIR DANS LES PIERRES

2

Soleil route usée pierres frémissantes
Une lance d'orage frappe le monde gelé
C'est le jour des liquides qui frisent
des liquides aux oreilles de soupçon
dont la présence se cache sous le mystère des triangles
Mais voici que le monde cesse d'être gelé
et que l'orage aux yeux de paon glisse sous lui
comme un serpent qui dort sa queue dans son oreille
parce que tout est noir
les rues molles comme des gants
les gares aux gestes de miroir
les canaux dont les berges tentent vainement de saluer les
     nuages
et le sable
le sable qui est gelé comme une pompe
et projette au loin ses tentacules de cristal
Tous ses tentacules n'arriveront jamais à transformer le
     ciel en mains
Car le ciel s'ouvre comme une huître
et les mains ne savent que se fermer sur les poutres des mers
qui salissent les regards bleus des squales
voyageurs parfumés
voyageurs sans secousses
qui contournent éternellement les sifflements avertisseurs des
     saules
des grands saules de piment qui tombent sur la terre comme des plumes

℀ *SLEEPING SLEEPING IN STONES*

2

Sun rough road shuddering stones
A storm's spear hits the frozen world
It's the day when liquids curl up
liquids with suspicious ears
whose presence is hidden under the mystery of triangles
But now the world stops being frozen
and the storm with peacock's eyes slides under it
like a snake sleeping with its tail in its ear
because everything is dark
streets soft as gloves
stations with mirrorlike gestures
canals whose banks try vainly to greet the clouds
and the sand
the sand which is frozen like a pump
and projects far out its tentacles of crystal
All its tentacles will never succeed in transforming the
    sky into hands
For the sky opens up like an oyster
    and hands only know how to clasp onto beams of the sea
which soil the blue glances of sharks
perfumed travelers
unshaken travelers
who eternally skirt the warning whistles of willows
tall red pepper willows that are falling on the ground like
    feathers

Si quelque jour la terre cesse d'être un saule
les grands marécages de sang et de verre sentiront leur ventre
    se gonfler
et crier Orties Orties
Jetez les orties dans le gosier du nègre
borgne comme seuls savent l'être les nègres
et le nègre deviendra ortie
et soutane son oeil perdu
cependant qu'une longue barre de cuivre se dressera comme
    une flamme
si loin si haut que les orties ne seront plus ses enfants
mais les soubresauts fatals d'un grand corps d'écume
salué par les mille crochets des eaux bouillantes
que lance le pain blanc
ce pain si blanc qu'à côté de lui le noir est blanc
et que les roches amères dévorent lentement les chevilles des
    danseuses d'acajou

mais les orties ô mosaïque les orties demain auront des
    oreilles d'âne
et des pieds de niege
et elles seront si blanches que le pain le plus blanc s'oubliera
    dans leurs dédales
Ses cris retentiront dans les mille tunnels d'agate du matin
et le paysage chantera Un Deux Trois Quatre Deux Trois
    Un Quatre
les corbeaux ont des lueurs d'église
et se noient tous les soirs dans les égouts de dieu

Mais taisez-vous tas de pain le paysage lève ses grands bras
    de plume
et les plumes s'envolent et couvrent la queue des collines
et voici que l'oiseau des collines se retrouve dans la cage de
    l'eau

Mais plumes arrêtez-vous car le paysage n'est presque plus
    qu'une courte paille
que tu tires
C'est donc toi fille aux seins de soleil qui seras le paysage
l'hypnotique paysage
le dramatique paysage
l'affreux paysage
le glacial paysage

If someday the earth ceases to be a willow
the large swamps of blood and glass will feel their bellies
    swell
and cry Nettles Nettles
Throw the nettles in a nigger's gullet
one-eyed as only niggers can be
and the nigger will become a nettle
and his lost eye a cassock
meanwhile a long bar of copper will stand up straight as
    a flame
so far so high that the nettles will no longer be his children
but fatal convulsions of a great body of foam
greeted by a thousand hooks of seething waters
that the white bread throws
that bread so white that next to it black is white
that the bitter rocks slowly devour the ankles of mahogany
    dancing girls

but the nettles oh mosaic the nettles tomorrow will have
    donkey's ears
and feet of snow
and the nettles will be so white that the whitest bread will go astray
    in their labyrinths
Its cries will resound in the morning's thousand agate tunnels
and the landscape will sing One Two Three Four Two Three
    One Four
crows have church gleams
and drown every night in god's gutters

But be quiet heap of bread the landscape is lifting its long
    feather arms
and the feathers fly off and cover the tail of the hills
and now the bird from the hills finds itself in the
    water's cage

But feathers stop for the landscape is now hardly more than a short
    straw
that you draw
So it's you girl with breasts of sun who will be the landscape
the hypnotic landscape
the dramatic landscape
the frightful landscape
the glacial landscape

l'absurde paysage blanc
qui s'en va comme un chien battu
se nicher dans les boîtes à lettres des grandes villes
sous les chapeaux des vents
sous les oranges des brumes
sous les lumières meurtries
sous les pas hésitants et sonores des fous
sous les rails brillants des femmes
qui suivent de loin les feux follets des grands hérons du jour
    et de la nuit
les grands hérons aux lèvres de sel éternels et cruels
éternels et blancs
cruels et blancs

4

Nue nue comme ma maîtresse
la lumière descend le long de mes os
et les scies du temps grincent leur chanson de charbon
car le charbon chante aujourd'hui
le charbon chante comme un liquide d'amour
un liquide aux mouvements de volume
un liquide de désespoir

Ah que le charbon est beau sur les routes tournesol
tournesol et carré
si je t'aime c'est que le sol est carré
et le temps aussi
et cependant je ne ferai jamais le tour du temps
car le temps tourne comme à la roulette
la boule qui regarde
dans la mosaïque des forêts

Cerveaux et miroirs roulez
Car le charbon a la tête d'un dieu
et les dieux ô cerises les dieux aujourd'hui plantent des
    épingles
dans le cou des zouaves
et les zouaves n'ont plus de moustaches
parce qu'elles accompagnent les jets d'eau
dans la course de l'avoine

the absurd white landscape
that goes away like a beaten dog
to curl up in the mail boxes of big cities
under hats of the winds
under oranges of the mists
under damaged lights
under hesitant and sonorous steps of madmen
under shining rails of women
we follow from afar the will-o'-the-wisps of the tall herons
    of the day and night
the tall herons with lips of salt eternal and cruel
eternal and white
cruel and white

4

Nude nude like my mistress
the light descends along my bones
and the saws of time grind out their coal song
for the coal is singing today
the coal is singing like a love liquid
a liquid with voluminous movements
a liquid of despair

Oh how lovely is the coal on sunflower roads
sunflower and square
if I love you it's because the earth is square
and time also
and yet I'll never go all around time
for time turns like the ball on a roulette wheel
that looks
into the mosaic of forests

Brains and mirrors roll on
For the coal has the head of a god
and the gods oh cherries the gods today are
    planting pins
in the necks of zouaves
and the zouaves no longer have mustaches
because the mustaches go with the fountains
in the oat race

l'avoine cirée lancée le long des vents à la poursuite des
	marées
Marées de mes erreurs où mîtes-vous nos vents
car vos vents sont aussi des marées
ô mon amie
vous qui êtes ma marée mon flux et mon reflux
vous qui descendez et montez comme le dégel
vous qui n'avez de sortie que dans la chute des feuilles
et ne songez point à vous échapper
car s'échapper c'est bon pour une flèche
et les flèches qui s'échappent ont frôlé tous les soupirs
mais vous qui êtes dans l'eau comme un remous
belle comme un trou dans une vitre
belle comme la rencontre imprévue d'une cataracte et d'une
	bouteille

La cataracte vous regarde belle de bouteille
la cataracte gronde parce que vous êtes belle
bouteille
parce que vous lui souriez et qu'elle regrette d'être cataracte
parce que le ciel est vêtu pauvrement
à cause de vous dont la nudité reflète des miroirs
vous dont le regard tue les vents malades
Mon amie ma fièvre et mes veines
je vous attends dans le cercle le plus caché des pierres

et malgré la lance du dramatique navire
vous serez près de moi qui ne suis qu'un point noir
Et je vous attends avec le sel des spectres
dans les reflets des eaux volages
dans les malheurs des acacias
dans le silence des fentes
précieuses entre toutes parce qu'elles vous ont souri
comme sourient les nuages aux miracles
comme sourient les liquides aux enfants
comme sourient les traits aux points

waxed oats thrown along the winds in pursuit of
    tides
Tides of my errors where did you put our winds
for your winds are also tides
oh lover
you who are my tide my ebb and flow
you who go up and down like the thaw
you who have no way out except in the fall of leaves
and don't ever dream of escaping
for escaping is good for an arrow
and arrows that escape have brushed every sigh
but you who are in water like an eddy
beautiful as a hole in a windowpane
beautiful as the unexpected meeting of cataract
    with bottle

The cataract looks at you beautiful by bottle
the cataract grumbles because you are beautiful
bottle
because you smile at it and because it's sorry about being a cataract
because the sky is poorly clothed
on account of you whose nudity reflects mirrors
you whose glance kills sick winds
My lover my fever and my veins
I'm waiting for you in the innermost circle of stones
and in spite of the dramatic ship's lance
you will be close to me I who am only a black dot
and I wait for you with the salt of ghosts
in the reflection of inconstant waters
in the misfortune of acacias
in the silence of crevices
precious above all because they smiled at you
as clouds smile at miracles
as liquids smile at children
as dashes smile at periods

❧ *LE GRAND JEU*

S'essouffler

À Max Morise

Ah fromage voilà la bonne madame
Voilà la bonne madame au lait
Elle est du bon lait du pays qui l'a fait
Le pays qui l'a fait était de son village

Ah village voilà la bonne madame
Voilà la bonne madame fromage
Elle est du pays du bon lait qui l'a fait
Celui qui l'a fait était de sa madame

Ah fromage voilà du bon pays
Voilà du bon pays au lait
Il est du bon lait qui l'a fait du fromage
Le lait qui l'a fait était de sa madame

Réforme

En traîneau sur la Néva
je glisse translucide
entouré d'hippocampes blancs
Petit cul pâle
que viens-tu faire ici
les casse-noisettes ont fermé leurs oreilles
les champignons poussent sur la fonte
Il n'y a plus que nous qui pensons aux gommes à effacer

❧ THE BIG GAME

Getting Out of Breath *
To Max Morise

Oh cheese there's the good lady
There's the good milk lady
She's made of good milk from the country that made it
The country that made it was from her home town

Oh town there's the good lady
There's the good lady cheese
She's from the country with good milk that made it
The one that made it was from her lady

Oh cheese there's some good country
There's some good milk country
It's from the good milk that made it from cheese
The milk that made it was from her lady

Reform

By sleigh on the Neva
I'm sliding translucent
surrounded by white sea horses
Pale little ass
what are you doing here
the nutcrackers have closed their ears
the mushrooms are growing on the thawing snow
We alone still think of erasers

* This poem is based on a popular song.

Portrait de Paul Éluard

Les dents sombres montent sur les étoiles
Quelles étoiles
Une voix éclate sur le gazon meurtri
comme une fesse
Quelles fesses
Le vent couvre les cheveux des semences
Les semences passeront
mais tes nuages ne passeront pas
J'en ai un dans ma poche
qui s'élèvera jusqu'à ma bouche
alors je sourirai à tes étoiles

C'est gai hein

Le Sang et les arrêts

Petite vaisselle
aboutira
Beurre d'oiseau
grandira
Pelle de sel
patinera
Citron maudit
se mariera
Gazelle verte
s'éventera
Cigare de nuage
s'encanaillera
Grande poussière
se développera
Manège de soie
dormira
Patère mélancolique
se balancera
Groseille fauve
flambera

Portrait of Paul Éluard

Dark teeth climb on the stars
What stars
A voice cries out on the lawn bruised
like a buttock
What buttocks
The wind covers the seeds' hair
The seeds will pass on
but your clouds will not
I have one in my pocket
which will rise clear up to my mouth
Then I'll smile at your stars

That's funny huh

Blood and Arrests

Little dish
will end up
Bird butter
will grow
Salt scoop
will skate
Cursed lemon
will marry
Green gazelle
will spoil
Cloud cigar
will go bad
Big dust
will develop
Silk merry-go-round
will sleep
Melancholy coathook
will rock
Tawny currant
will go up in flames

Flamme solide
tressaillera
Carte à oreilles
bourgeonnera
> *Mais le jeune explorateur qui les mains vides franchit*
l'enceinte où le premier né les pieds joints le coeur avide
et la cervelle cousue ravive l'incident lointain qui rendit
impossible l'élection de la meule souveraine
> *Ainsi elle se pose jambes en l'air épaules lointaines et*
mains partout mains multipliées par le détour et le roman
découvert sous le chapeau
> *On bout on trempe dans la rue comme dans un baquet*
d'acide on se gonfle comme une aubergine on s'assoupit
comme une bûche qui brûle on se meuble comme une cuvette
Alors le marbre glisse long des jambes mortes et s'étale sur
l'équateur comme une petite flaque sonore

Le Langage des saints

Il est venu
il a pissé
Comme il était seul
il est parti
mais il reviendra
l'oeil dans la main
l'oeil dans le ventre
et sentira
l'ail les aulx
Toujours seul
il mangera les asperges bleues des cérémonies officielles

Le Mariage des feuilles

L'homme découvre la poésie circulaire
Il s'aperçoit qu'elle roule et tangue
comme les flots de la botanique
et prépare périodiquement son flux et son reflux

Solid flame
will quiver
Map with ears
will bud
But the young explorer who empty-handed scaled the wall where the
first-born feet together heart eager and brain stitched up tight revives
the long past incident that made the election of a sovereign haystack
impossible
Thus the haystack settles legs in the air shoulders far-off and
hands everywhere hands multiplied by the detour and the novel discovered
under the hat
Everyone boils everyone soaks in the street as in a tub of acid
everyone swells up like an eggplant everyone dozes off like a burning
log everyone furnishes themselves like a washbowl Then the marble slides
along dead legs and stretches out on the equator like a little deep-toned puddle

The Language of Saints

He came
he pissed
As he was alone
he left
but he will return
an eye in his hand
an eye in his belly
and will smell a clove
of garlic cloves of garlic
Still alone
he will eat the blue asparagus of official ceremonies

The Leaves' Marriage

Man discovers circular poetry
He sees that it pitches and rolls
like botanical tides
and periodically prepares its ebb and flow

O saints que n'êtes-vous ceints de seins sains
Votre seing figureait une main de pouces
agitée d'un tremblement alcoolique
O saints qu'avez-vous sur la main
Est-ce une main plus petite
que recouvre une autre main plus petite
et ainsi jusqu'à la consommation des mains

La poussière s'agite dans sa solitude
Elle veut que le silence qui l'entoure
se peuple de fantômes ailés
aux voix de trones pourris
de femmes légères comme la dame blanche
de vieillards descendus de la montagne
en proie aux nieges éternelles
des grandes montagnes molles
où tournent virent et plongent
les chaussons de danse

Un Oiseau a fienté sur mon veston salaud
À Pierre Naville

Main vide et pied levé
le bon enfant sur deux assiettes
mourait d'envie de rire d'un cheval
solitaire
de la lune
de la rousse
Au lieu de mourrir
il aurait pu rire
il préféra cogner comme un sourd
sur l'arbre le plus proche
L'arbre miaulait
T.S.F. T.S.F.
La T.S.F. le mordit au pied droit
et un ours à la main gauche
Comme il était jeune il n'en mourut pas
On le décora
on en fit un ambassadeur
Paul Claudel

Oh saints if only you were girdled with healthy breasts
Your signature would picture a hand of thumbs
beset by an alcoholic shake
Oh saints what do you have in your hand
Is it a smaller hand
that covers another smaller hand
and so on up to the consummation of hands

The dust is restless in its solitude
It wants the surrounding silence
to be peopled with winged phantoms
with voices of decayed trunks
of women light as the white lady
of old men come down from the mountain
tormented by the eternal snows
of the great soft mountains
where dancing slippers
turn swing round and dive

A Bird Has Shit on My Jacket Son of a Bitch

To Pierre Naville

Empty-handed with his foot raised
the good child on two plates
was dying to laugh about a horse
one lone horse
about the moon
about the cops
Instead of dying
he could have laughed
he preferred to bang like a deaf man
on the closest tree
the tree was meowing
Radio Radio
The radio bit him on the right foot
and a bear on the left hand
As he was young he did not die from it
He was decorated
He was made an ambassador
Paul Claudel

Ils étaient de connivence

Que dit l'arc-en-ciel du vagin
au petit sauvage
habillé de vert-de-gris

Le vagin était nu
comme le sauvage

Il n'avait plus l'âge de mentir
moins encore de gémir
moins encore de chatouiller
le nombril du village voisin
Hé hé
Ce n'est pas prudent
pensait le village voisin
Sait-on jamais
si du nombril
les derniers couvercles
allaient jaillir comme un mâle
sans être précédés d'une lanterne
qu'est-ce qui ne rirait plus

La Boîte aux lumières

Elle est pleine d'un coton léger
qui s'envole au moindre bruit
qui crépite au moindre vent
qui s'ennuie à la moindre pluie
et qui tue pour le moindre désir

Cela ne peut pas continuer ainsi
Il tombe sur les pieds de mon voisin
une mousse de nuages
qui est verte
Ce sont des épinards

Il tombe sur la tête de ma voisine
des cailloux de fourrure
dont elle fait ses délices
Ce sont des souris

They Worked in Collusion

What did the vagina's rainbow
say to the little savage
dressed in verdigris

The vagina was nude
and so was the savage

It was no longer young enough to lie
still less to groan
still less to tickle
the navel of the neighboring village
Ho ho
That's not a good idea
thought the neighboring village
Do you ever really know
whether out of the navel
the last lids
might squirt out like a male
without a lantern in front of them
what wouldn't laugh any more

The Box of Lights

It is full of light cotton
which flies off at the slightest sound
which crackles at the slightest breeze
which is bored at the slightest rain
and which kills at the slightest whim

It can't go on like this
On the foot of the man next to me is falling
a moss of clouds
which is green
It's spinach

On the head of the woman next to me are falling
pebbles of fur
which she delights in
They are mice

Le Quart d'une vie

I

À l'intérieur
le catalogue vendait des huîtres vivantes
qui pleuraient et qui chantaient
sur un air américan

II

Les feuilles qui sont tombées
ont emporté les deux taxis
Les taxis ont renversé les sémaphores
Les sémaphores tombés
le lait ne coulera plus
car les moustaches tombées
ne repousseront plus

III

Nous sommes plus heureux que la mousse
la mousee n'a pas de cheveux
et nous portons des chapeaux
Pauvres chapeaux aux ailes couvertes de givre
la fumée des cigarettes vous excite
mais le pétrole
le pétrole sournois qui vide les ostensoirs
est plus léger à vos reins
que les chaînes d'aluminium

IV

Croupissez regards des sulamites
Il pleut Il neige
Sous le soleil qui nous déteste
les chiens mangent la merde
les ceinturons s'enrichissent des sabots des vieux
     chevaux
qui les oreilles percées
le ventre lumineux
vendent leurs chemises aux portes des églises
sans se soucier des cachalots et des zébus
Joli mois d'août c'est le mois des zébus

A Quarter of a Lifetime*

I
Inside
the catalog was selling live oysters
which were crying and singing
an American tune

II
The fallen leaves
have swept off two taxis
The taxis have knocked over traffic lights
Since the traffic lights have fallen
milk will no longer flow
for the fallen mustaches
will no longer grow

III
We are happier than moss
the moss hasn't any hair
and we are wearing hats
Poor hats with frost-covered wings
cigarette smoke excites you
but kerosene
the crafty kerosene that empties ostensories
is lighter on your back
than aluminum chains

IV
Wallow sulamite glances
It's raining It's snowing
Under the sun that hates us
dogs eat shit
sword-belts grow rich from old horse hooves
which with their ears pierced
with luminous bellies
sell their shirts near church doors
without worrying about cachalots and zebus
The fine month of August is zebu month

* This form of poem, reviewing one's life, is reminiscent of medieval verse, in particular the poetry of François Villon, whose iconoclastic spirit resembles Péret's in many respects.

Les zébus ont trop bu
bu bu bu et boira
boira qui voudra
mais ce n'est pas moi qui le voudrai
C'est trop laid le cervelet
qui sans sourire court à la chapelle
téléphoner aux parfumeurs

V

C'est un jour saint un jour sacré
un jour sacré à l'hôtel
Vivent les atlas sous les bateaux

VI

Plutôt que périssent les cannibales
nous démolirons les pianos
nous interdirons les vendanges
nous arrêterons les marées

VII

Couverture des étoiles
le vent roule des motocyclettes
Il ne croit pas à l'eau salée
et symbolise les aspirations des peuples
comme la guerre
comme les vêtements

VIII

La cavalerie n'est pas loin
et les oscillations non plus

IX

Vers le ciel de juillet
montent les fourrures ovipares
Le serrurier militaire
invente le contrepoint
nécessaire à la nourriture des abeilles

X

L'éléphant sans moteur
naquit sans scandale
Absalon-la-main-verte lui sourit
et rangea les lis de ses viscères
sur un poteau

The zebus have drunk too much
have drunk have drunk and will drink
whoever wants to will drink
but I don't want to
The cerebellum is too ugly
without a smile it runs to the chapel
to telephone the perfumers

V

It is a holy day a sacred day
a sacred day in the hotel
Long live the atlases under boats

VI

Rather than let the cannibals perish
we will demolish the pianos
we will prohibit the harvests
we will stop the tides

VII

Star cover
the wind drives motorcycles
It doesn't believe in salt water
and symbolizes the peoples' aspirations
like war
like clothes

VIII

The cavalry isn't far off
the oscillations aren't either

IX

Up to the July sky
fly oviparous furs
A military locksmith
invents the counterpoint
necessary for feeding bees

X

A motorless elephant
was born without scandal
Green-Handed-Absalom smiled upon him
and hung up the lilies of his viscera
on a pole

sur une épingle
Guetté par le scorbut
il sera veuf un jour
où la couleur changera comme la chaleur

XI

Noble coeur songe au collodion
qui les pieds dans ses cheveux
s'ennuie s'ennuie s'ennuie
comme un bouquet de lilas
dans une valise

XII

Miroirs de balcons
les balcons sur les citernes
évitent les avirons
invitent les kangourous
visitent les ailes des moulins
et meurent comme les zouaves
sans océan et sans chaussettes
Ainsi soit-il

XIII

Le visage roulé dans la farine
le tropique du Capricorne est dans ma main
qui tremble
qui s'amincit et s'allonge
qui roule
et s'en va très loin sous un arbre
comme un rat malade

XIV

Vins et cheminée
allons nous-en
Nos pieds ont leurs épingles
et les veaux leur mystère
Sans ministre ni harpon
allons nous-en

XV

Il est temps de vous marier
si vous craignez la pluie
vieux monastère sans ceinture

on a pin
Watched by scurvy
he'll be a widower some day
when color will change like heat

XI

A noble heart contemplates collodion
with its feet in its hair
it is bored bored bored
like a bouquet of lilacs
in a suitcase

XII

Mirrors on balconies
balconies on cisterns
avoid oars
invite kangaroos
visit sails of windmills
and die like zouaves
without the ocean and without socks
So be it

XIII

Its face rolled in flour
the Tropic of Capricorn is in my hand
which is shaking
which is growing thin and long
which is rolling
and goes far away under a tree
like a sick rat

XIV

Wines and hearth
let's go away
Our feet have their pins
and the calves their mystery
Without a minister or a harpoon
let's go away

XV

It's time to get married
if you are afraid of rain
old beltless monastery

plaques grises
coton de malheur

XVI

Alors de la gouttière
un membre mal fermé
dont le nom mal brossé
dégoulinait sur un poisson
s'enflamma sans dégoût
Sa destinée fut courte comme une sueur
Ma soeur
as-tu vu ma pipe
Ma pipe est morte
et mon grand oeil est sans saveur

gray plates
bad-luck cotton

      XVI
So from the gutter
an unlatched limb
on which the uncombed name
trickled out over a fish
caught fire without disgust
Its destiny was as short as a sweat
Dear sister
have you seen my pipe
My pipe is dead
and my wide eye is dreary

❧ JE NE MANGE PAS DE CE PAIN-LÀ

Louis XVI s'en va à la guillotine

Pue pue pue
Qu'est-ce qui pue
C'est Louis XVI l'oeuf mal couvé
et sa tête tombe dans le panier
sa tête pourrie
parce qu'il fait froid le 21 janvier
Il pleut du sang de la niege
et toutes sortes de saletés
qui jaillissent de sa vieille carcasse
de chien crevé au fond d'une lessiveuse
au milieu du linge sale
qui a eu le temps de pourrir
comme la fleur de lis des poubelles
que les vaches refusent de brouter
parce qu'elle répand une odeur de dieu
dieu le père des boues
qui a donné à Louis XVI
le droit divin de crever
comme un chien dans une lessiveuse

La Stabilisation du franc

Si les oreilles des vaches frémissent
c'est qu'on chante la *Marseillaise*
Allons enfants de la tinette
morver dans l'oreille de Poincaré

❧ I WON'T SWALLOW THAT

Louis XVI Goes off to the Guillotine

Stinks stinks stinks
What stinks
It's Louis XVI the unhatched egg
his head is falling into the basket
his rotten head
because it's cold this 21st day of January
It's raining blood and snow
and all sorts of filth
spurting from his old carcass
a dead dog's carcass in a washtub
tangled in dirty laundry
which has had time to rot
like the fleur-de-lis in garbage cans
which cows refuse to eat
because it gives off a smell of god
god the father of mud
who gave Louis XVI
the divine right to die
like a dog in a washtub

The Stabilization of the Franc

If cows' ears are shaking
it's because people are singing the Marseillaise
Come children of the johns
Slobber in Poincaré's ear

Les macaronis attardés dans sa barbe
ont beau murmurer
C'est moi le nouveau franc
À bas le vieillard qui m'a fait bouillir
Comme un carton à la foire
l'oeil dans le vase de nuit
Poincaré se répète
J'ai bien mérité de la tinette
Vive l'union des bourriques
Vive la vacherie nationale

6 Février

Vive le 6 février
grogne le jus de chique
vêtu en étron fleurdelysé

Que c'était beau
Les autobus flambaient comme les hérétiques d'autrefois
et les yeux des chevaux
arrachés par nos cannes-gillettes
frappaient les flics si répugnants et si graisseux
qu'on aurait dit des croix de feu

Vive le 6 février
J'ai failli incendier le ministère de la marine
comme un kiosque à journaux
Dommage que les pissoitières ne brûlent pas

Vive le 6 février
Des conseillers municipaux abrutis par leur écharpe tricolore
pour rallier les poux et les punaises
faisaient couler leur sang sous les matraques
qui leur conviennent moins bien que le poteau d'exécution

The macaroni lingering in his beard
murmurs in vain
I am the new franc
Down with the old man who made me boil
Like a target at a fair
his eye in a chamber pot
Poincaré talks to himself
I certainly deserve the john
Long live the union of asses
Long live the national pigsty

The Sixth of February *

Long live the sixth of February
grumbles the tobacco juice
dressed in shit adorned with fleur-de-lis

How fine it was
Buses were burning like heretics in the old days
and horses eyes
torn out by our cannes-gillettes**
were hitting the cops who were so disgusting and fat
that you'd think they were Croix-de-feu

Long live the sixth of February
I almost set fire to the Ministry of the Marine
like a newsstand
Too bad that public urinals don't burn

Long live the sixth of February
Some town-councilmen besotted by their tricolor sashes
trying to rally the lice and bedbugs
were shedding their blood with bludgeons
which were far less fitting than an execution stand

* This poem is based on a parliamentary crisis, connected with the Stavisky affair, in 1934. On February 6, there were riots and an attempted coup by the right wing. The "Croix-de-feu" was a right-wing veterans' organization that took part in the six riots. Although this expression is not capitalized in the poem, it is possibly the allusion Péret intended.

** Word with no English translation; probably a sharp, makeshift weapon.

Vive le 6 février
Des curés jaunes verts pourris
caressaient les fesses des adolescents
en chantant la *Marseillaise* et des cantiques
en tirant sur leurs frères flics

Vive la 6 février
et vive le 7
j'ai hurlé pendant deux jours
À mort Cachin À mort Blum
et j'ai volé tout ce que j'ai pu dans les magasins
dont je brisais les vitres
j'ai même volé une poupée que j'enverrai à Maurras
pour qu'il essaie de la violer
en criant À bas les voleurs

Long live the sixth of February
Some yellow green rotten priests
were caressing boys' asses
while they sang the Marseillaise and some hymns
and shot their fellow cops

Long live the sixth of February
and long live the seventh
I shouted for two days
Death to Cachin Death to Blum
and I stole everything I could in the stores
breaking the windows
I even stole a doll which I'll send to Maurras
so he can try to rape it
shouting Down with the thieves

DE DERRIÈRE LES FAGOTS

Quatre à quatre

Meurtrie par les grandes grues électriques
la patte de mouche voyage cependant dans mon oeil comme
nul explorateur
Qu'il pleuve des sardines
ou vente à en tirebouchonner le Mont Blanc
elle voyage sans se laisser arrêter par la tentation des
parapluies fermés
vieux sabres de panoplies
qui ne savent plus que se moucher et éternuer
Se moucher et éternuer
en voilà une vie que n'envieraient pas les carottes à la
sauce blanche
ni l'herbe qui pousse entre les pavés bordés de dentellières
sournoises comme un oeil derrière un lorgnon
comme un signal de chemin de fer qui passe du rouge au
vert
sans plus crier gare
qu'un jardin public où se cache un satyre
Mais la patte de mouche ne demande rien à personne
car les professeurs ne craignent que les escaliers branlants
où le gaz réussit parfois à tuer son ennemi le rat
à coups de pierres comme un flic chassé à courre
et les étoiles qui effraient les poissons rouges
ne sont ni à vendre ni à louer
car à vrai dire ce ne sont pas des étoiles mais des tartes aux
abricots
qui ont quitté la boutique du pâtissier
et errent comme un voyageur qui a perdu son train à minuit

❧ FROM BEHIND THE WOODPILE

Four by Four

Bruised by the tall electric cranes
the fly's foot still travels around my eye better than any explorer
Whether it's raining sardines
or blowing hard enough to twist Mont Blanc
it is traveling and resists the temptation of closed-up umbrellas
old sabre trophies
which now can only blow their noses and sneeze
Blow their noses and sneeze
that's a life envied neither by carrots in cream sauce
nor the grass that grows between paving stones bordered by lacemakers
cunning as an eye behind a lorgnette
as a train signal changing from red to green
without any more warning
than a public park where a satyr hides
But the fly's foot doesn't ask anybody anything
because professors only fear loose stairs
where gas sometimes manages to kill its enemy the rat
by throwing stones like a cop being routed out
and the stars that frighten red fish
are neither for sale nor for rent
for to tell the truth they aren't stars but apricot pies
that have left the pastry shop
and are wandering like a traveler who has lost his train at midnight

dans une ville déserte aux becs de gaz geignant à cause
de leurs vitres cassées
Même si le voyageur rencontre une femme nue marchant
sur le bord du trottoir
parce qu'entre les maisons et elle passe un troupeau
silencieux
de crocodiles épouvantés par le feu de leurs pipes
et cherchant une église avec un large bénitier
même si le voyageur rencontre cette jeune femme
il n'évitera pas l'incendie d'un magasin de confections
d'où s'enfuiront des milliers de puces qui seront tenues pour
responsables du désastre
mais si le magasin brûle comme une lampe Pigeon
le voyageur se sentira consolé
et attendra
paisiblement
bêtement
amoureusement
courageusement
tristement
ou paresseusement
que sa barbe pousse pour se raser
et se fera une large entaille près de l'oreille
par où sortira prudent et inquiet
un petit lézard de verre
qui ne réussira jamais à retrouver le nombril de son maître
et se perdra dans la cheminée
où l'attendent pour lui faire un mauvais parti
l'épingle à cheveux l'épingle à chapeau l'épingle de cravate
l'épingle de nourrice
et cette brute de saladier écorné
qui serre déjà les poings

Chasse à courre

Je m'étonne de l'orthographe de *fois*
qui ressemble tant à un champignon
roulé dans la farine

in a deserted city with gas lamps groaning because
    of their broken panes
Even if the traveler meets a nude woman walking
    along the edge of the sidewalk
because between her and the houses is passing a
    silent herd
of crocodiles terrified by the smoke from their pipes
looking for a church with a wide holy-water basin
even if the traveler meets that young woman
he won't avoid the clothing store on fire
from which thousands of lice will flee who will be held
    responsible for the disaster
but if the store burns like a Coleman lantern
the traveler will be comforted
and will wait
peacefully
stupidly
lovingly
courageously
sadly
or lazily
for his beard to grow so he can shave
and will make a wide cut near his ear
out of which will come careful and anxious
a little glass lizard
which will never manage to find its master's navel again
and will get lost in the fireplace
where lying in wait to kill him are
the hairpin the hatpin the tiepin the safety pin
and that brute of a cracked salad bowl
already clenching its fists

The Hunt

The spelling of *fois* surprises me*
It looks so much like a mushroom
rolled in flour

---

* The word *fois* can be simply translated as "time." I have left it in the original, however, because there is a roundness suggested by the phonetic group (*wa*) in French that somehow better suits the visual image of a mushroom that Péret immediately develops.

Il n'a pas les mains blanches parce qu'il est nègre
Son nez est une boussole
qui se retourne vers le centre
où il fait chaud
C'est le creux de ma main
Il crache sur le soleil qui a froid
et veut me voler mon pardessus
qui n'a rien à se mettre sous la dent

À Mi-chemin

Le vieux chien et la puce ataxique
se sont rencontrés sur le tombeau du soldat inconnu
Le vieux chien puait l'officier crevé
et la puce disait
Si ce n'est pas malheureux de s'accrocher des petites merdes
      avec des rubans rouges
sur la poitrine
Jadis les poireaux pourris ne rougissaient pas d'être
      pourris
les bouts de bois toussotant et crachotant
faisaient des corbillards très convenables
avec une odeur vénéneuse de champignons d'église
et la moustache ne servait qu'à balayer
Maintenant les sources de vieux poils jaillissent entre les
      pavés
et tu les adores vieux général
car ils viennent du crâne d'un curé
qui n'a pas d'os
qui n'a pas d'yeux
et qui se regarde dissoudre dans un bénitier

Mille fois

À Elsie

Parmi les débris dorés de l'usine à gaz
tu trouveras une tablette de chocolat qui fuira à ton
      approche
Si tu cours aussi vite qu'un tube d'aspirine

It doesn't have white hands because it's Negro
Its nose is a compass
that turns in towards the center
where it's warm
It's the palm of my hand
It spits on the sun which feels cold
and wants to steal my overcoat
which has nothing to eat

Halfway

The old dog and the ataxic flea
happened to meet on the tomb of the unknown soldier
The old dog stank like a dead officer
and the flea said
Isn't it too bad to pin little bits of shit with red ribbons
on your chest
Formerly rotten leeks didn't blush about being rotten
coughing and spitting bits of wood
made very respectable hearses
with a poisonous odor of church mushrooms
and the mustache was only used for sweeping
Now springs of old hair shoot up between cobblestones
and you simply adore them old general
for they come from the skull of a priest
who hasn't any bones
who hasn't any eyes
and who watches himself dissolving in a holy-water basin

A Thousand Times
To Elsie

In the golden debris of the gas factory
you'll find a chocolate bar that will flee when you come close
If you run as fast as a tube of aspirin

tu iras loin derrière le chocolat
qui bouleverse le paysage
à la manière d'un soulier percé
sur lequel on jette un manteau de voyage
pour ne pas effrayer les passants par le spectacle de cette
     nudité
qui fait claquer des dents aux boîtes de poudre de riz
tomber les feuilles des arbres comme les cheminées
     d'usine
Et le train passe sans s'arrêter devant une petite gare
parce qu'il n'a ni faim ni soif
parce qu'il pleut et qu'il n'a pas de parapluie
parce que les vaches ne sont pas encore rentrées
parce que la route n'est pas sûre et qu'il n'aime pas
recontrer des ivrognes ou des voleurs ou des flics
Mais si les alouettes faisaient la queue à la porte des
     cuisines
pour se faire rôtir
si l'eau refusait de couper le vin
et si j'avais cinq francs
Il y aurait du nouveau sous le soleil
Il y aurait des pains à roulettes qui défonceraient les casernes
     de gendarmerie
Il y aurait des pépinières de barbe où les moineaux feraient
     l'élevage des vers à soie
il y aurait dans le creux de ma main
un petit lampion froid
doré comme un oeuf sur le plat
et si léger que la semelle de mes chaussures s'envolerait
     comme un faux nez
en sorte que le fond de la mer serait une cabine
     téléphonique
d'où personne n'obtiendrait jamais aucune communication

Faire des pieds et des mains

L'oeil levé l'oeil couché l'oeil assis

Pourquoi s'égarer entre deux haies de rampes d'escalier
pendant que les échelles s'assoupissent

you'll go far behind the chocolate
which upsets the landscape
like a shoe with a hole in it does
on which a travel-coat is thrown
so as not to frighten passersby with the spectacle
        of its nudity
which makes the powder boxes' teeth chatter
which makes the leaves on the trees fall like factory smokestacks
And the train goes by without stopping in front of a little station
because it isn't hungry or thirsty
because the weather's rainy and it doesn't have an umbrella
because the cows haven't come home
because the road isn't safe and it doesn't like
to meet drunkards or thieves or cops
But if larks would stand in line in front of kitchen doors
to be roasted
if water would refuse to dilute wine
and if I had five francs
There would be something new under the sun
There would be bread on roller skates which would break into
        the gendarmes' barracks
There would be nurseries for beards where sparrows would raise silkworms
in the palm of my hand there would be
a cold little Chinese lantern
gilded like a fried egg
and so light that the sole of my shoes would fly away
        like a false nose
so that the ocean floor would be a
        telephone booth
from which no one could ever make a call

To Do One's Utmost

One eye up one eye down one eye seated

Why get lost between two rows of staircases
while ladders drowse

comme des nouveau-nés
comme les zouaves qui perdent leur patrie avec leurs
    chaussures
Pourquoi lever les bras au ciel
puisque le ciel s'est noyé
sans rime ni raison
pour passer le temps et faire pousser ses moustaches
Pourquoi mon oeil s'assied-il avant de se coucher
parce que les bâts blessent les ânes
et que les crayons se brisent de la plus imprévisible façon
par tous les temps
à l'exception des jours d'orage
où ils se brisent en zigzags
et des jours de neige
où ils déchirent leur chandail
Mais les lunettes les vieilles lunettes dépolies
chantent en cueillant du chiendent pour les chats
Les chats suivent la troupe
en portant des drapeaux
des drapeaux et des insignes
L'arête de poisson qui traverse un coeur battant
la gorge qui se soulève régulièrement pour imiter la mer
    qui l'entoure
et le poisson qui tourne autour d'un ventilateur
Il y a aussi des mains
de longues mains blanches avec des ongles de verdure
    fraîche
et des phalanges de rosée
des cils oscillants que contemplent des papillons
mélancoliques parce que le jour a fait un faux-pas dans
    l'escalier
Il y a aussi des sexes frais comme une eau vive
et qui bondissent dans la vallée
parce que le soleil les touche
Ils n'ont pas de barbe mais des yeux clairs
et poursuivent les libellules
sans se soucier du qu'en dira-t-on

like newborn babes
like zouaves who lose their country with their shoes
Why raise one's arms up to the sky
since the sky drowned
without rhyme or reason
to pass time and to let its mustaches grow
Why does my eye sit down before going to bed
because shoes pinch feet
and because pencils break most unpredictably
in all kinds of weather
except on stormy days
when they break in zigzags
and on snowy days
when they tear their sweaters
But spectacles old dull spectacles
sing while picking grass for the cats
the cats follow the troops
carrying flags
flags and badges
The fishbone that pierces a beating heart
the breast heaving regularly to imitate the sea around it
and the fish turning around an electric fan
There are hands too
long white hands with nails of fresh greenery
and phalanxes of dew
Fluttering eyelashes watched by butterflies
sad because the day stumbled in the stairway
There are also genitals fresh as quick water
leaping in the valley
because the sun touches them
They don't have beards but they do have bright eyes
and are chasing dragonflies
not worrying about what people will say

Atout trèfle

Assemble la pierre de l'élan brisé et l'erreur des branches
    au fil de l'eau
Doute de l'horizon de l'autre côté de tes yeux
et va-t-en à travers les montagnes blanches de fougères
que sapent lentement les cordelettes de la passion folle
Les cuisses du ciel s'arrondiront devant toi
et les ténèbres fermeront leur porte sans verrou
car le verrou ne se tire pas à cause des malfaiteurs en
    forme de tunnel
mais à l'unique voisinage des pentes abruptes
et lorsque les colliers de mirages se brisent comme le cristal
    des larmes
que le ruisseau s'affaisse lourdement comme un verre vide
le misérable coquillage de la route se déroulera comme une
    ceinture de sauvetage
une ceinture qui ne sauve que les suicidés aux mains de
    flamme
debout sur les collines qui rient
car les collines des suicidés rient d'un rire de chute d'eau
avec des vis dans leur voix de fumée
et des escaliers infinis dans leurs gestes
qui s'égarent dans les boules bleues du temps perdu
Celui qui n'a pas perdu son temps dans les soupapes de la
    neige
ne connaît pas la force dissolvante de l'aubépine fleurie
    baignant dans le sable blond
ni le courage désespéré des petites rivières traversant des
    marais d'armoiries
Et celui qui n'a pas senti le regard prismatique des
    palmiers
se poser sur l'épine dorsale de l'avoine
dont la chute correspond au degré de torréfaction du café
celui-là ne sait pas ce que c'est que le vent perdu
et ne peut prétendre qu'à l'oubli
au plus définitif oubli des cils battants
à moins que son souffle sursaute
au passage affolé des murailles mordues par les écorces
    tombantes
qu'anime la colère des obstacles surmontés

Clubs Trump

Gather the stone whose force is broken together with the error of branches
    in the current
Doubt the horizon beyond your eyes
and go off across the white mountains of ferns
slowly sapped by strings of mad passion
The thighs of the sky will round out before you
and the shadows will close their door that has no bolt
for the bolt can't be drawn on account of evildoers in
    the form of a tunnel
but only in proximity of steep slopes
and when mirage necklaces break like the crystal of tears
when the stream sinks heavily like an empty glass
the miserable shell on the road will unfold like a life belt
a belt which saves only suicide victims with hands of flame
standing on hills which laugh
for the suicide victims' hills are laughing the laugh of a waterfall
with screws in their smoky voices
and infinite stairs in their gestures
which are lost in the blue spheres of lost time
He who has not lost his time in the valves of snow
does not know the solvent force of the flowering hawthorn
    bathing in blond sand
nor the desperate courage of little rivers crossing
    bogs of armorial bearings
And he who has not sensed the prismatic glance of
    palm trees
cast on the wheat's spine
whose fall corresponds to the degree of roasting for coffee
that person does not know what the lost wind is
and can only aspire to oblivion
to the total oblivion of fluttering lashes
unless his breath leaps up with a start
when terrorized walls pass bitten by
    falling rinds
enlivened by the anger of obstacles overcome

Qui est-ce

J'appelle tabac ce qui est oreille
et les mites en profitent pour se jeter sur le jambon
d'où un remarquable combat entre les sources
jaillissant du pain d'épices
et les lunettes qui empêchent les aveugles de voir clair
Même si la femme en face de moi mangeait une table de
      dissection
la roulette donnerait des déboires à un prince chinois
qui se cache dans une valise
dans laquelle un vagabond ganté et botté
comme un porte-plume
reconnaîtrait facilement l'arc-en-ciel qui apparaît loin
      au-dessus des vignes après la vendange
quand le vin hésite à devenir rouge ou blanc
et renonce à tout jamais à regarder l'avenir en face
de peur que celui-ci lui tourne le dos
en sifflant une tyrolienne
où il serait question de cheveux blonds
à moins que ce ne soit de cheveux bruns
ou bien de lièvres qui tuent les perdrix
pour que la chasse soit bonne
et que le vent qui souffle dans les cheminées
empêche les rivières de dormir dans leur lit

Who Is It

I call tobacco that which is ear
and the moths take advantage of it to attack the ham
a remarkable fight ensues between the springs
gushing from the gingerbread
and the glasses that prevent blind people from seeing clearly
Even if the woman opposite me should eat a dissection table
the roulette wheel would rebuff a Chinese prince
who is hiding in a suitcase
in which a vagabond with gloves and shoes
like a penholder
would easily recognize the rainbow which appears
    far above the grapevines after the harvest
when the wine hesitates to become red or white
and refuses ever after to face the future squarely
for fear that the latter will turn its back on him
whistling a Tyrolian tune
about blond hair
unless it might be about brown hair
or else about hares that kill partridges
so that the hunt will be good
and so that the wind that blows down chimneys
will prevent rivers from sleeping in their beds

❧ JE SUBLIME

Allo

Mon avion en flammes mon château inondé de vin du Rhin
mon ghetto d'iris noirs mon oreille de cristal
mon rocher dévalant la falaise pour écraser la garde-
    champêtre
mon escargot d'opale mon moustique d'air
mon édredon de paradisiers ma chevelure d'écume noire
mon tombeau éclaté ma pluie de sauterelles rouges
mon île volante mon raisin de turquoise
ma collision d'autos folles et prudentes ma plate-bande
    sauvage
mon pistil de pissenlit projeté dans mon oeil
mon oignon de tulipe dans le cerveau
ma gazelle égarée dans un cinéma des boulevards
ma cassette de soleil mon fruit de volcan
mon rire d'étang caché où vont se noyer les prophètes
    distraits
mon inondation de cassis mon papillon de morille
ma cascade bleue comme une lame de fond qui fait le
    printemps
mon revolver de corail dont la bouche m'attire comme l'oeil
    d'un puits
scintillant
glacé comme le miroir où tu contemples la fuite des oiseaux
    mouches de ton regard
perdu dans une exposition de blanc encadrée de momies
je t'aime

❧ MYSELF SUBLIME

Hello

My plane on fire my castle flooded with Rhine wine
my ghetto of black iris my crystal ear
my rock rushing over the cliff to crush the town policeman
my opal snail my air mosquito
my bird-of-paradise down quilt my black foam hair
my tomb burst wide open my shower of red grasshoppers
my flying island my turquoise grape
my collision of crazy and careful cars my wild flowerbed
my dandelion pistil shot into my eye
my tulip bulb in the brain
my gazelle lost in a theater on the boulevards
my sun box my volcano fruit
my laughter like a hidden pond where absentminded prophets
    drown themselves
my flood of cassis my morel butterfly
my waterfall blue as a ground swell that makes spring come
my coral revolver whose mouth attracts me like the eye
    of a well
sparkling
cold as the mirror where you gaze at the flight of your hummingbird
    glances
lost in an exhibition of white framed by mummies
I love you

Parle-moi

Le noir de fumée le noir animal le noir noir
se sont donné rendez-vous entre deux monuments aux morts
qui peuvent passer pour mes oreilles
où l'écho de ta voix de fantôme de mica marin
répète indéfiniment ton nom
qui ressemble tant au contraire d'une éclipse de soleil
que je me crois quand tu me regardes
un pied d'alouette dans une glacière dont tu ouvrirais la porte
avec l'espoir d'en voir s'échapper une hirondelle de pétrole
    enflammé
mais du pied d'alouette jaillira une source de pétrole flambant
si tu le veux
comme une hirondelle
veut l'heure d'été pour jouer la musique des orages
et la fabrique à la manière d'une mouche
qui rêve d'une toile d'araignée de sucre
dans un verre d'oeil
parfois bleu comme une étoile filante réfléchie par un oeuf
parfois vert comme une source suintant d'une horloge

Source

Il est Rosa moins Rosa
dit la giboulée qui se réjouit de rafraîchir le vin blanc
en attendant de défoncer les églises un quelconque jour de
    Pâques
Il est Rosa moins Rosa
et quand le taureau furieux de la grande cataracte m'envahit
sous ses ailes de corbeaux chassés de mille tours en ruines
quel temps fait-il
Il fait un temps Rosa avec un vrai soleil de Rosa
et je vais boire Rosa en mangeant Rosa
jusqu'à ce que me j'endorme d'un sommeil de Rosa
vêtu de rêves Rosa
et l'aube Rosa me réveillera comme un champignon Rosa
où se verra l'image de Rosa entourée d'un halo Rosa

Talk to Me

The blackness of smoke the animal blackness black blackness
made a date between two monuments for the dead
which can pass for my ears
where the echo of your sea mica ghost's voice
repeats your name indefinitely
which looks so much like the opposite of an eclipse of the sun
that you'd open
hoping to see a swallow made of burning oil fly out
the door of the icebox where I think I'm a skylark's foot when you look at me
but from the lark's foot will gush forth a spring of flaming oil
if you wish
as a swallow
likes the summertime to play storm music
and invents it like a fly
that dreams of a sugar spider's web
in a glass eye
sometimes blue as a falling star reflected by an egg
sometimes green as a spring oozing from a clock

Source

It's a quarter to Rosa
said the hailstorm pleased to refresh the white wine
while waiting to wreck the churches one ordinary Easter Day
It's a quarter to Rosa
and when the mad bull from the great cataract overtakes me
under its crow-wings chased from a thousand towers in ruins
what kind of weather is it
It's Rosa weather with a real Rosa sun
and I'm going to drink Rosa eating Rosa
until I go to sleep in a Rosa sleep
dressed in Rosa dreams
and dawn Rosa will awaken me like a mushroom Rosa
where I'll see Rosa's image wreathed in a Rosa halo

❧ UN POINT C'EST TOUT

Un Matin

Il y a des cris à n'en plus finir
des braillements de terre agitée comme un éventail démantelé
par des taupes en conserve
des sanglots de planches qu'on étripe
longs comme une locomotive qui va naître
des convulsions d'arbres révoltés qui ne veulent pas plus
     laisser monter la sève
que le métro n'accepte de transporter des autruches
dans ses tunnels de barbe mal rasés
il y a des cris
des araignées de vitriol que j'avale sans m'en apercevoir
près de ce fleuve usé issu d'un tuyau de pipe
qui n'est autre qu'un long museau
un peu chaud
un peu plus grognon qu'un chaudron presque vide
ce fleuve que tu ne vois pas plus que la poussière d'une hostie
que le vent a mélangée
à la poussière du curé semblable à du sulfate de cuivre
et à celle de l'église plus tordue qu'un vieux tire-bouchon
car tu n'es pas plus là que je ne suis là sans toi
et le monde en est tout dépeigné

✖ ONE POINT AND THAT'S ALL

One Morning

There's no end of shouts
bawls from the earth as agitated as a fan dismantled
by canned moles
sobs from boards being gutted
long as a locomotive about to be born
convulsions of trees in revolt which do not want to let their sap rise
any more than the subway wants to carry ostriches
in its tunnels full of stubble
there are cries
from the vitriol spiders which I swallow unawares
near that worn-out river coming from a pipe-stem
which is none other than a long snout
somewhat warm
somewhat more peevish than an almost empty cauldron
that river which you can see no better than the dust of a host
which the wind has mixed
with priest's dust similar to copper sulfate
and with church dust more twisted than an old corkscrew
for you are no more here than I am here without you
and so the world is all disheveled

❧ À TÂTONS

Mille regrets

Du fond du granit qui cache son secret de lichen
sous un clinquant de saltimbanques
encerclant une équipe de lutteurs transis de froid
sous leur vêtements de pince à épiler
émerge une lueur triste de lampe à pétrole qui serait une
    chatte
guettant les cicatrices essoufflées du mur
ermite barbu qu'une vaste plaine plantée de conques marines
rapproche des troncs qui l'ont banni
mais isole des banques dont les cloches qu'il n'entend pas
hantent son sommeil peuplé de hanches
flottant dans un vent d'aurore qui lui rend des satins mats
dont la teinte se ravivera vite
pourvu que la chatte esquisse le pas des lanciers
devant sa proie satisfaite d'une goutte d'eau venue de si loin
qu'elle s'affaisse épuisée par la fatigue
de tant de passages du chaud au froid
que l'accordéon expire dans ses bras en projetant un dernier
    jet de vinaigre
indispensable à la multiplication des feuilles
qui répètent l'heure à tous les échos
tordues par un vent à raser de près
et habitées par des ressorts qui se tendent et se détendent
au rythme d'une valse qu'on n'entend pas
parce qu'elle est fredonnée si bas
par des orties si hautes qu'on dirait des mâts de cocagne
    énervés par le dernier printemps

❦ GROPING

Awfully Sorry

From the depths of the granite that keeps its lichen secret
under a clowns' show of tinsel
surrounding a team of wrestlers frozen cold
under their clothes of tweezers
emerges a kerosene lamp's sad light which could be a cat
lying in wait for the breathless scars on the wall
bearded hermit whom a vast plain planted with sea shells
reunites with the trunks that banished him
but isolates from the banks whose bells which he doesn't hear
haunt his sleep peopled with haunches
floating in a dawn wind that dulls satins
whose color will be quickly restored
provided that the cat mimics a lancer's step
in front of its prey satisfied by a drop of water come from so far away
that it collapses dead beat
from so many changes from hot to cold
provided the accordion expires in its arms emitting a final
        squirt of vinegar
indispensable to the multiplication of leaves
which strike the hour always echoing
twisted by a close-shaving wind
and inhabited by springs coiling and uncoiling
to the rhythm of a waltz no one can hear
because it is hummed so low
by nettles so high you'd think they were Maypoles *
        weakened by last spring

* "Mâts de cocagne" are poles set up in a village square for games. Maypoles are not for the
same game but reflect a similar spirit of country life and pleasure.

et qu'elle se perd dans leur vengeance
en tablier blanc
et en bottes de sept lieues
pour mieux persécuter les calèches aux joues flasques
qui gémissent du matin au soir
comme des litres

Le Premier jour

À l'intérieur de la lettre *a* germe le doigt sur les lèvres
car le *b* s'abat sur la tête du *c*
qui éclate et répand autour d'elle une odorante résine
d'où s'échappent des soupirs gravissant quatre à quatre les
      échalas du désir
cependant que le *d* ivre
titube et s'écroule dans un escalier abrupt
au pied duquel il se retrouve *j* rongeant les souliers de *g*
qui nu et couvert de poils des pieds à la tête
se baigne dans la paisible rivière *q*
sans crainte des nénuphars hypocrites qui le guettent
pour l'étrangler comme un *f* innocent
dont la disparition passera inaperçue
jusqu'à ce qu'un *i* s'envole à tire-d'ailes de chaque corolle
pour former un lumineux soir de printemps
incitant les *e* à s'attarder sur le seuil de leur porte
miroitant des mille cris des *n* épouillant à qui mieux mieux
un long panache qui disparaît dans son puits coutumier
où l'attend un *l* souriant dont les seins de fer de lance
marquent une mesure qui s'apaise seulement
dans les bras de rochers recélant d'avides coquillages
que parfois *r* lui tend comme un pont franchissant une gorge
hantée de fantômes épouvantés qui se bousculent et se
      piétinent
à qui le premier se saisira du flambeau étincelant
emporté par un *h* écumant d'une rage des premiers âges
vers les grands déserts tapissés de squelettes qui s'élèvent
      en tourbillons
dès que *p* soupire comme un clin d'oeil furtif à l'adresse
      d'une passante
dont la silhouette de caresses légères s'évanouit déjà

and because it is lost in their vengeance
wearing a white apron
and seven-league boots
the better to persecute the slack-jawed carriages
groaning from morning to night
like liters

The First Day

Inside the letter *a* is sprouting a finger on the lips
for *b* is pouncing on the head of *c*
which bursts and spreads an odorous resin
from which escape sighs climbing four by four the
     trellis of desire
while *d* drunk
staggers and falls down a steep staircase
at the foot of which it finds itself changed into *j* gnawing the shoes of *g*
which nude and hairy from tip to toe
is swimming in the peaceful river *q*
undaunted by the hypocritical waterlilies lying in wait
to strangle it like an innocent *f*
whose disappearance will pass unnoticed
until an *i* flies swiftly off from each corolla
to form a luminous spring evening
inciting the *e*'s to linger on their doorstep
flashing thousands of cries from the *n*'s vying with each other to delouse
a long plume disappearing into its usual well
where a smiling *l* is waiting for it whose breasts of spearheads
beat a rhythm which slows down only
in the arms of rocks concealing eager shellfish
which *r* sometimes hands it like a bridge crossing a gorge
haunted by terror-stricken ghosts jostling and trampling each other
to see who will first grab the flashing torch
carried off by an *h* fuming with primordial rage
to great deserts hung with skeletons rising in whirlwinds
as soon as *p* sighs like a furtive wink at a woman passing by
whose silhouette of light caresses is already vanishing

entre les pages d'un vieux roman d'amour
feuilleté avidement à l'ombre de *t*
qui ne verra pas l'horreur toujours attendue
jamais surmontée
des tas de *k* sanglotant à ses pieds
jour en spirale affolée et nuit de malle bourrée à éclater
et suppliant un implacable *o* de leur épargner la honte
des cultures de primeurs
fourmillant d'*m* voraces dont la morsure venimeuse
les jette dans une lente agonie
où insensibles aux brûlantes piqûres des *v*
qui les traversent peu à peu pour se rejoindre et célébrer
     leur fête annuelle
à l'abri des grands *s* qui protègent leurs ébats
cependant qu'au loin un *u* armé de pied en cap
livre un duel à mort a l'*x* qu'il immolera
malgré les reproches amers de *w* que la colère aveugle
Mais *y* calme aux grands yeux de ruine veille et le retient
Il était temps car *u* se retourne et menace
Assez *w* ou je te *z*

Sans autre formalité

Reçu de la marée montante une grande vague à oeillères
presque sèche
mais frétillante et ronronnant d'aise
d'être arrivée au terme d'un voyage qui l'a réduite de
     moitié
et la laisse le plumage hérissé
jaune et plein de vermines qui jouent du violoncelle
sans rime ni raison
car la sirène appelant les ouvriers au travail
provoque l'arrêt de leur coeur supérieur
dont les ressorts en se brisant
démolissent toute leur mécanique intérieure
ce qui lisse les plumes de la vague
maintenant rassurée
les rend à leurs études mathématiques
cependant que la vague entreprend incontinent la culture
     des yeux

between the pages of an old love story
leafed through avidly in the shadow of *t*
which will not see the horror always expected
never overcome
of piles of *k*'s sobbing at its feet
by day in wild spirals by night trunks filled to bursting
and beseeching an implacable *o* to spare them the shame
of fresh produce
teeming with voracious *m*'s whose venomous bite
precipitates them into a slow agony
where insensitive to the burning stings of *r*'s
which pierce them bit by bit to gather together and celebrate
    their annual reunion
safe from the big *s*'s which protect their revels
while in the distance a *u* armed from head to toe
wages a death duel with the *x* it will immolate
despite the bitter rebuke of *w* blinded by anger
But *y* calm wide-eyed with ruins stands by and restrains it
It was high time for *u* turns and threatens
That's enough *w* or I'll *z* you

Without Further Ado

Received from the incoming tide a great wave with blinders
nearly dry
but quivering and purring with pleasure
having arrived at the end of a trip that half consumed it
leaving its plumage bristling
yellow and full of lice that play the cello
without rhyme or reason
for the siren calling the workers back to work
provokes the arrest of their superior heart
whose springs breaking
destroy their entire inner mechanism
all that smooths the feathers of the wave
now reassured
leaves them to study their math
while the wave undertakes forthwith the production of eyes

avec des cils de vols de colibris
qui donnent des regards transformant les échines
en cristal vibratile
rendant l'interminable son aigu
d'une tour qui s'envole d'un seul coup d'aile
jusqu'aux neiges éternelles qu'elle arrache de leur demeure
pour en vêtir sa toute récente pudeur
qui ne lui permit plus de contempler le soleil face à face
Reçu

with lashes of flocks of hummingbirds
which cast glances transforming the spines
into vibratile crystal
making the interminable sharp sound
of a tower flying off with one wing beat
up to the eternal snow it tears from home
to clothe its new-found modesty
which no longer lets it gaze at the sun face to face
Received

✣ AIR MEXICAIN

Air mexicain

Le feu vêtu de deuil jaillit par tous ses pores
La poussière de sperme et de sang voile sa face tatouée de
    lave
Son cri retentit dans la nuit comme l'annonce de la fin des
    temps
Le frisson qui se hâte sur sa peau d'épines court depuis que
    le maïs se lisse dans le vent
Son geste de coeur brandi à bout de bras s'achève en
    cinquante-deux ans dans un brasier d'allégresse
Lorsqu'il parle la pluie d'orage excite les réflexes des lueurs
    enfouies sous la cendre des anciens rugissements que les
    lions de feu lancent en s'ébrouant
Il écoute et n'entend couler que le torrent de sa sueur d'or
    avalée par le Nord noir
Il chante comme une forêt pétrifiée avec ses oiseaux sacrifiés
    en plein vol dont l'écho épuisé traîne le ramage qui va
    mourir
Il respire et dort comme une mine cachant sous des douleurs
    inouïes ses joyaux de catastrophe

Quand l'aile chatoyante de l'aube se perdait dans les gouffres
    du crépuscule habité de gestes mous
quand les larmes du sol éclataient en gerbes infernales
    d'années sans nuits
les cierges s'allumaient de toutes leurs griffes à futur sang
    fidèle
pour que plonge dans un sommeil vidé de rêves d'ancêtres
    exigeants

🦋 *MEXICAN AIR*

Mexican Air

Fire in mourning spurts from every pore
Dust of sperm and blood covers his face tattooed with lava
His cry echoes in the night like the sign of the end of time
The shudder in haste on his thorny skin has been running since the corn
    has been preening in the wind
His heartfelt gesture brandished at arms length ends after fifty-two
    years in a blazing mass of joy
When he speaks the rain excites gleams buried under the ashes of timeless
    roars hurled by fire lions tossing
He listens and hears only the torrential flow of his golden sweat drunk
    by the black North
He sings like a petrified forest with birds sacrificed in full flight whose
    spent echo prolongs a warbling doomed to die
He breathes and sleeps like a mine hiding its jewels of disaster under
    unparalleled pain

When the dawn's shimmering wing was lost in the gulfs of twilight
    peopled with soft gestures
when the earth's tears burst into showers of infernal
    nightless years
tapers lit up with all their claws of faithful future blood
so that the master of life who curses the maws that slaver
    his vital flame

le maître de la vie qui jette des injures aux gueules bavant
    la flamme qui l'anime
pour que l'homme trouve là-haut la route des grands miroirs
    d'eau bruissants de lances de lune
et là-bas des ciels de lit qui chantent un air de jeune fille
    revenant de la fontaine mouchetée de vols paresseux et
    flasques où deux yeux luisent comme la paroi suintante
    d'une caverne qui attend la vie
Nul n'aurait pu dire où commençait la mer puisque les
    fleuves rentraient dans l'oeuf que Tlaloc rosée qui ne
    s'était pas fait reconnaître ne cachait pas encore dans
    sa gueule de tigre
Cependant dans la nuit vagissante le regard du nouvel an
    vient de s'allumer à celui de l'aigle qui pique vers le sol
Nouvel an à facettes de cristal où le profane ne découvre
    qu'une trombe de poussière aspirant des échos calcinés
    par un dieu toujours vainqueur
et des parole noyées dont le corps momifié flotte flotte et
    s'envole d'un coup d'aile dans un rais de lumière qui
    s'éteignant les rejettera sur la terre pour qu'elles
    donnent des fruits d'obsidienne
Les hommes jaillissaient de l'ombre comprimée à l'ouest du
    rayon vert une graine à la main comme un fantôme aux
    yeux
Il est temps disaient-ils que la terre secoue sa chevelure
    vivante selon le rythme des airs du jour en pyjama
que nous descendions cajoler la grenouille retrouvée après
    tant de soleils d'oubli châtiés par les quatre éléments
que l'or et l'argent du ciel la parent d'un collier de plumes
    à étancher les soifs rebelles comme les paupières
    entr'ouvertes d'un ruisseau racontant les rêves de sa
    source
que de la chrysalide du limon s'échappe le papillon qui
    contient et emporte notre cri automnal à reflets de
    lendemains déguisés en monstres
que la poussière de la voie lactée n'ait plus à tomber d'aussi
    haut puisque les mille doigts de notre mère la recueillent
    au passage
que la griffe de mortification répande son lait aigre de bête
    dissimulée sous des pierres d'avalanche dont sa vie de
    fantôme exalté fécondera la nôtre quatre à quatre

would fall into a sleep free from dreams about exacting ancestors
so that man would find on high the road with great mirrors of water
        murmuring moon spears
and below canopies of beds singing the song of a young girl
        returning from a fountain spotted with lazy flaccid flights where
        two eyes gleam like the sweating wall of a cave awaiting life
No one could say where the sea began since the rivers were
        running back into the egg that rosy Tlaloc* himself still
        undisclosed was not yet hiding in his tiger's gullet
Yet in the howling night the new year's gaze has just now been kindled
        by the gaze of the eagle diving down towards earth
The new year with crystal facets where the profane can only see a whirlwind of
        dust sucking in echoes burnt to a cinder
        by an ever-victorious god
and drowned words whose mummified bodies float float and then take
        wing flying into a ray of light which dimming will leave them
        stranded on earth so they may bear fruits of obsidian
Men burst forth from the shadow confined to the west of the
        green ray each with a seed in his hand like a ghost
        with eyes
It is time they said for the earth to shake its living hair
        to the rhythm of songs of the day in pyjamas
for us to go down and coax the frog rediscovered after
        so many forgotten suns scourged by the four elements
for heaven's gold and silver to adorn that frog with a necklace
        of feathers to quench thirsts as stubborn as the half-closed
        eyelids of a stream relating the dreams of its source
for the clay's chrysalis to give birth to a butterfly that will
        contain and bear our autumnal cry with shades of
        future days disguised as monsters
for the milky way's dust no longer to be obliged to fall from
        such a height since our mother's thousand fingers catch it going by
for the claw of mortification to spread its sour milk come from beasts
        hidden under avalanche stones with which its impassioned
        ghost life will make our life fruitful four by four

---

* Tlaloc is a Mexican rain god.

que la montagne à chevelure d'astre vengeur reconnaisse
    l'enfant que nous édifierons au bord du lac où nous a
    chassé la grande marée de son ennemi tantôt vainqueur
    tantôt vaincu
que le jour soit comme le visage du voisin et réponde à
    l'appel de son nom découvert par les savants de la
    gomme
que la pierre brille d'un éclat d'eau dont les lourdes
    paupières se ferment à cause du regard insoutenable
    d'un ciel que n'ose violer aucun oiseau
qu'elle fredonne l'air miraculeux des quatre points
    cardinaux qui nous protégeront contre l'égarement
    du chien poursuivant éternellement sa queue
qu'elle supplie les géants tapis sous la terre les eaux le feu
    et nos gestes qui les créent comme un plat succulent
qu'elle menace en leur nom les fourbes tyrans des déserts
    et de l'ombre qui étrangle avec le délire de ses vols
    noirs
D'où vient le cri qui ne chasse pas encore les bêtes des forêts
    poudrées par des ondes magnétiques
quel songe de père assassiné l'a fait ricocher d'île en rocher
    oublié par une terre exilée dans la nuit qu'elle hypnotise
Nul ne savait si la lueur d'accouchement qu'il poursuivait
    jusqu'à l'horizon terrifié par son audace s'envolerait
    au-dessus de lui ou plongerait dans la rainure zigzagante
    d'un plancher gelé
Nul ne savait qu'au raide et muet cadavre du blanc
    succéderait le refrain du vert qui s'éveille en se frottant
    les yeux de tous ses oiseaux
mais l'horreur du toit qui s'écroule et s'émiette sans mot
    dire les poussait vers les poissons acharnés à pénétrer
    le mystère des sources houspillées par des clartés
    inconnues
vers les étendues de viande bouillonnante dont l'effarement
    imite le galop de l'ombre s'avançant l'éclair à la main
vers le délire des branches tressant des prisons pour leurs
    folies à l'abri des esprits des profondeurs soulevés
    contre l'air pur
Et de tendre les bras vers les nuages qui défilent au pas de
    parade avec leur sourire provocant de demains lumineux
    comme un cristal à visage de fleurs écloses sous la rosée

for the mountain with the tail of a vengeful comet to recognize
        the child that we will edify on the shores of a lake where the
        great tide of its enemy now victorious now vanquished has driven
        us
for the day to be like the face of a neighbor and to answer when
        someone calls its name discovered by eraser scholars
for the stone to shine with the brilliance of water whose heavy
        eyelids droop on account of the unbearable stare
        of a sky that no bird dares violate
for the stone to hum a miraculous tune of the four points
        of the compass that will protect us against distractions
        like a dog eternally chasing its tail
for it to beseech the giants crouched under the earth the waters
        the fire and our gestures that create them like a succulent food
for it to threaten in their name the crafty tyrants from the deserts
        and the shadow that strangles in black flights of folly
Where does that cry come from not yet hunting the beasts of forests
        powdered with magnetic waves
what dream of a murdered father made it bound from rock to island
        forgotten by an earth that was exiled in the very night it hypnotizes
No one knew if the glimmer of birth it pursued
        to the horizon's edge terrified by its audacity would fly
        off above it or dive into the zigzagging crack
        of a frozen floor
No one knew that the stiff and dumb cadaver of a white
        would be followed by the refrain of a green waking rubbing
        its eyes with all its birds
but horror of the roof that wordlessly collapses crumbles
        drove them on toward fish eager to solve
        the mystery of sources screamed at by unknown lights
toward expanses of boiling meat whose alarm
        imitates the gallop of a shadow forging ahead torch in hand
toward the delirium of branches weaving prisons for their
        follies safe from spirits of the depths rising up
        against the fresh air
And to drive them to reach out toward clouds marching
        in parade step with a provocative smile of morrows luminous
        as a crystal with a face of flowers blossoming in the dew

Et de reconnaître le séjour de l'aube derrière la montagne
    fumante aux ailes insouciantes qui scintillent dans un
    soleil de vierge
les sept cavernes à ténèbres de siècles couverts de mousse
    où le chef de la dualité installa sa poussière de
    multiplication
Un jour disaient-ils se dressera en hommage à lente spirale
    de larme végétale la pyramide que caressera le soleil
    arrêté pour ronronner au-dessus de nous
et s'attardant à incendier les allées de mica qui prolongent
    l'eau mourant de soif où il ira songer à la rosée du
    matin
pendant que sa soeur toujours languissante fait le guet pour
    nous préserver des hurlements épouvantés de l'ombre
    qui fait trembler nos os
aussi lui dresserons-nous sa montagne pareille à un chien
    jappant au retour de son maître

Lorsque la lumière folle de rage échappe au flot de requins
    l'attaquant d'un appétit entretenu par des ripailles
    démesurées
une herbe la salue d'un papillon titubant qui la désigne pour
    l'offrande convoitée par des yeux que la crampe agrandit
C'est là que la terre à la toison bouillonnante d'ailes si
    épaisse qu'à peine les étincelles du bois fondant y
    peuvent exploser en fusées de fête et si haute qu'aucun
    chant n'en jaillit en stalagmite de joie vers le vide
    toujours innocent
que la terre a oublié depuis des milliers de brasiers
    reconnaissants qu'elle naquit semblable à un squelette
    jadis honoré d'assauts de curés crochus
qu'elle élève là vers un guerrier toujours triomphant et
    n'écoutant que son désir jamais comblé ses mains
    jointes à fourrure de faim apaisée
C'est juré L'éclair du quetzal fuyant vers son complément
    l'affirme comme un jour pur de toute crainte même
    détalant comme un voleur à l'horizon
Rien ni les bagarres féroces des monstres de la terre fondant
    les pierres dans leurs mains de soleil noir dont le
    sang de haute flamme déborde parfois en longs galops
    criminels ni l'haleine enfiévré des nuages écrasants
    ni leurs sanglots qui ne domine aucun ordre

to recognize the dawn's abode behind a smoking mountain
    with carefree wings that sparkle in a virgin's sun
the seven caves with shades of moss-covered centuries
    where the chief of dualism set up his multiplication dust
Someday they said in full honor a pyramid kissed by the sun slowed
    to purr above us will be raised in a plant tear's slow spiral
and stopping to set ablaze the avenues of mica that prolong
    the water dying of thirst where he will go to dream of the
    morning dew
while his sister always languishing lies in wait to save us from
    the terrified howls of the shadow shaking our bones
Thus will we build his mountain resembling a dog
    barking when his master returns

When the light mad with rage escapes from the school of sharks
    attacking him with an appetite whet by immoderate feasts
a blade of grass salutes it with a tipsy butterfly that designates
    it for the offering coveted by eyes opened wide in pain
There the earth with fleece seething with wings so thick that
    sparks of melting wood can scarcely explode as fireworks
    and so high that no hymn can burst out in joyful stalagmite
    toward the still-innocent void
there the earth has forgotten after thousands of grateful fires that
    it was born resembling a skeleton formerly honored by
    attacks from crooked priests
there it raises high to a warrior always triumphant and heeding
    only his unslaked desire clasped hands with fur of
    appeased hunger
Sworn to be true The flash of the quetzal* fleeing toward its
    complement recognizes it as a day pure of any fear running
    like a thief toward the horizon
Nothing neither fierce skirmishes of earth monsters melting stones
    in their hands of black sun from which high-flamed blood overflows
    at times in long criminal gallops nor the feverish breath of
    oppressive clouds nor their sobs where no order rules

---

*   The quetzal is a bird found in southern Mexico and the Central American countries that was
considered mythical and a symbol of liberty by the Aztecs. It was integrated in the image of the
plumed serpent, who also appears as a character in this poem, to represent the god Quetzalcoatl.

ni les becs obscurs aux mâchoires de cruauté qui étincellent
dans les haleines glauques et lancent leurs lémures à
résorber parce qu'ignorants du chant de la lumière
n'empêchera que l'herbe grandisse comme un génie
hallucinant et d'une banderole insouciante appelle
les hommes à recueillir ses pains de lumière à égrener
comme les jours d'une vie
rien n'empêchera plus que l'homme aux yeux fourmillant
de mirages entrevus ne la contemple comme son amante
aux seins qui se consument en un printemps étoilé de
promesses inépuisables
et dans un ballet d'âmes à peine nées et pourtant certaines
que leurs enfants peupleront le monde palpable comme
un arbre foudroyé et celui qu'on devine dans les
frémissements des ombres de cris croisant le fer et de
voix aimables aux visages hantés
Plus tard les lieux ayant reçu des *grands tapirs de l'aube* leur
face chantante ou hostile selon le sort jeté par un rayon
bienveillant ou un souffle hargneux
la terre se réjouissant des êtres qui émergeaient à sa surface
de bébé satisfait comme des bulles d'air colorées par le
rapace dans sa chute
les hommes ayant appris à connaître les voix obscures comme
une subtile reptation dans la forêt qui tend son oreille
épanouie et les rires clairs comme une goutte d'eau qui
tombe de feuille en fleur avec son paradis prisonnier
le tigre de la pluie réclamait son festin d'hosties enchantées
d'une fin glorieuse le grand-père du feu son cadeau
de fleurs à parfum de coeurs palpitants et la fée du maïs
sa couronne de rosée où se miraient les montagnes
surveillées par leur génie qui passait de la paix des
prairies et des bois après l'orge aux rages écumantes
d'enfer débordant en moins de temps que le jour n'en
prend pour coiffer sa cagoule
et le puits de son regard intérieur appelait sa vierge ravie
de porter aux dieux la prière haletante de la tribu et
lui promettait un remède de miracle aux calamités d'une
saison de haines imméritées
Le Nord en deuil perpétuel déjà rejetait ses vagues d'êtres
sans visage et sans voix toujours avides d'air neuf et
les blocs écroulés des demeures chères aux maîtres des

nor obscure beaks with cruel jaws sparkling in the glaucous breath
        and casting their lemurs to be reabsorbed because they know
        nothing of the song of light
nothing will prevent the grass from growing like a hallucinating
        spirit and calling forth with a carefree streamer the men to
        harvest its loaves of light to be counted off one by one like
        the days in a lifetime
now nothing can prevent man his eyes teeming with half-seen mirages
        from contemplating the earth like his mistress with breasts
        consumed in a springtime starred with endless promises
and in a ballet of souls newborn yet sure that their children will
        people one world as tangible as a lightning-struck tree and
        another seen in the shudders of the shadows of cries crossing
        swords and of friendly voices with haunted faces
Later when the faces of the earth receive from the *dawn's great tapirs*
        their own look singing or hostile according to the fate cast by a
        kindly beam or an ill-tempered gust of wind
the earth rejoicing in the creatures emerging on its surface babyishly
        satisfied like air bubbles colored by a bird of prey in its fall
when men had learned to recognize voices obscure as a subtile creeping
        in the forest lending a wide-open ear and laughter clear as a drop
        of water falling from leaf to flower with its captive paradise
the rain tiger demanded its feast of hosts enchanted by a glorious end
        the grandfather of fire his gift of flowers smelling like beating
        hearts and the corn fairy her crown of dew in which were mirrored
        mountains guarded by their spirit who went from the peace of the
        prairies and woods after the barley to the hell-foaming furies
        brimming over in less time than the day takes to don its hood
and the well of its inner gaze called its virgin eager to bear
        the tribe's breathless prayer to the gods and promised her
        a miraculous remedy for the calamities of a season of
        undeserved hate
The North in perpetual mourning already cast out its waves of
        faceless and voiceless creatures always seeking new air and
        the blocks of stone fallen from dwellings dear to the universal

désirs de l'univers se redressaient pour d'autres génies
enragés que la plante à chevelure d'épousée calmait de
son sourire sans cesse renaissant comme l'étoile du
serpent à plumes
Le feu nouveau brillait rythmiquement Treize fois les
années du silex de la maison du lapin et du roseau
s'engendraient mutuellement comme le cri appelle
l'écho heureux de sa vie d'insecte suspendu au-dessus
d'un nuage liquide buvant midi
De l'oeil qui éveille pour mieux endormir était descendu le
serpent à plumes blanc et barbu offrant comme jadis au
sommet des monts d'adoration à la lumière et à l'ombre
valsant toute la vie les couleurs vivantes créées par leur
souffle d'or et d'argent alterné
Mais le miroir fumant roulant sur des coeurs présentés aux
siens arrive d'un seul bond des cités trop sacrées par
l'oubli pour qu'on y vive là où les deux mers saisissent
la corne d'abondance de leurs mains qui veulent se
joindre pour supplier l'écorché de revenir à l'heure
promise
et la vapeur de sang fiévreux qui le précède d'une
haleine de volcan donne un vertige exaltant comme
l'accomplissement d'un destin deviné aggravé par un
lait d'étoile qui pénètre d'un jet de fumée gonflant ses
voiles les têtes à cervelle de métal nouveau-né
Hors d'ici ombre des virgules chantantes la voix du sang
brumeux parle un langage d'arc-en-ciel

Le premier jour je serai ton fils à naître dans quatre ans
le second l'ombre pâle du maïs sortant de la grenouille
comme l'eau d'une source
le troisième le songe de duvet verdoyant que je t'ai envoyé
cette nuit
et le quatrième mon coeur décoloré ne battra plus que pour
toi
Tu me prendras quatre fois dans tes bras de sol qui soupire
après l'orage
A la première je te donnerai l'aube prenant son bain
à la seconde le cri du printemps vainqueur au jeu de pelote
à la troisième le piment de mes lèvres jamais éteintes
te dira que je reste ta victoire au combat et ton prisonnier
qui la chantera jusqu'à la mort

masters of desire rose up for other angry spirits which the
   plant with bride's hair calmed with its smile endlessly reborn
   like the star of the plumed snake
The new fire blazed rhythmically Thirteen times the silex years of
   the house of the rabbit and the reed were mutually self-
   begotten as the cry calls out to the echo glad for its insect's
   life hung above a liquid cloud imbibing noontime
From the eye that awakens the better to put to sleep had come down
   the bearded white plumed serpent on top of the hills of
   adoration making offerings as of old to lights and shadows
   waltzing lifelong the living colors created by their breath
   alternately gold and silver
But the smoking mirror rolling on hearts that were gifts to its
   family arrives with a leap from cities made too sacred by
   oblivion for men to inhabit where two seas hold the horn of
   plenty in their hands wishing to clasp together so as to pray
   the flayed man to return at the promised time
and the vapor of feverish blood leading with the breath
   of volcanoes creates a dizziness as exhilarating as the
   fulfillment of a predicted destiny aggravated by a
   starry milk that penetrates with a blast of smoke filling
   its sails the heads with brains of newborn metal
Get out shadow of singing commas the misty blood's voice
   speaks a rainbow tongue

The first day I will be your son to be born in four years
the second the pale shadow of corn coming out of a frog
   like water from a spring
the third the dream of greening down that I sent you that night
and the fourth my faded heart will now beat only for you
Four times you will take me in your arms of earth that
   sighs after the storm
The first time I will give you the dawn bathing
the second the cry of spring winning a game of pelote
the third the red pepper of my never extinguished lips
   will tell you that I remain your victory in battle and your
   prisoner who will sing of it until death

à la quatrième j'aurai ton rire d'oiseau qui fuit la flèche
mais à la cinquième j'abandonnerai l'oeuf éclos l'an passé
des têtes sourdes comme des champignons larmoyants
et m'envolerai chez l'aigle qui tombe en avalanche
Tu ne pèseras pas plus qu'un brouillard sans queue ni tête
et rampant pour effacer les honneurs qui me sont dus
N'insiste pas comme l'ouragan qui rebondit de val en pic
tu n'auras plus que mon souffle pour t'endormir sur les
      vagues furieuses de la terre
comme une algue agonisante avec son corail captif
si bien qu'à l'oeil s'entr'ouvrant il ne restera plus que la
      coquille de ton corps

Le serpent à plumes s'en retourne méditer chez lui laissant
      son cri qui bondit de la neige à la fumée repart du maïs
      et s'arrête au signal de la méduse alors que le séjour de
      toute naissance s'éclaire d'un vagissement de pistil
      emporté par le vent
Les dieux sont allés hiverner au coeur des hommes et
      attendent en muant que les sauvages nouveau-nés des
      forêts qui les soutiennent arrivent à les prendre pour les
      hisser au sommet d'un nuage pyramidal
Deux fois les flammes ont emplumé les cimes en deuil sans
      que le colibri sorcier ait encore vu celui que roussit
      son maître dévorer un glissement venu du plus profond
      d'une nuit sans seigneurs
Ce n'est guère que le fond du lac pressé d'écouter les pas des
      tribus qui déjà se concentrent pour repartir aussitôt
      conquérir le commencement et la fin de l'eau les sources
      de l'orage et le dernier refuge de l'éclair
Ils arrivent du berceau des hérons d'aurore et marchent
      pendant que les années se nouent d'elles-mêmes en
      deux bottes d'asperges décapitées
L'oiseau sorcier né tout armé de la vierge à la jupe de
      serpents repousse d'une étincelle ses quatre cents
      ennemis excités par les souffles des ténèbres tenaces
      renaissant comme l'oeil s'ouvre et se ferme de leur
      cadavre toujours prêt à le harceler
Il les conduit avec la certitude des torrents appelés par leur
      apothéose vers la plante aux disques perfides narguant
      Tlaloc sur qui se donne le spectacle prophétisé d'un
      mythe de monde naissant

the fourth I will have your laugh of a bird escaping an arrow
but the fifth I will abandon the egg hatched last year
out of heads as deaf as tearful mushrooms
and will fly away to the nest of the eagle falling like an avalanche
You will be as light as a mist without head or tail
crawling to wipe out honors due me
Don't ask for more like the hurricane rebounding on hill and in vale
you will have nothing more than my breath to put you to sleep on the
    wild waves of the earth
like dying seaweed with its captive coral
so that seen by my half-opened eye only your body's shell will remain

The plumed serpent goes home to meditate leaving its cry which
    leaps from the snow to the smoke jumps off again from the
    corn and stops on a signal from the jellyfish when the
    realm of all births lights up with the wailing of pistils
    borne off by the wind
The gods went to hibernate in men's breasts and while moulting
    wait for the newborn savages from forests nurturing them
    to come take them and lift them up to the summit of a pyramidal cloud
Twice flames have feathered the peaks in mourning without
    the sorcerer hummingbird seeing the cloud scorched by his
    master devour a landslide come from the deepest
    of lordless nights
Hardly anything but the lake bottom urgently waits to hear the
    footsteps of the tribes that are gathering already only
    to leave soon to conquer the beginning and the end of the
    water the storm's source and the lightning's last shelter
They come from the cradle of the herons of dawn and march
    while the years tie themselves up in two bunches of
    headless asparagus
The sorcerer bird born fully armed from a snake-robed virgin fights off
    with a spark his four hundred enemies aroused by gusts from the
    tenacious gloom reborn as an eye opens and closes from their
    cadavers ever-ready for torment
It leads them with the certainty of rushing streams called by their
    apotheosis to the plant with falsehearted discs flouting
    Tlaloc in whose honor is performed a rite prophesying the
    myth of a world to come

Ici vivront dans leur demeure nimbée de sang les vrais chefs
    du jour et de la nuit aztèques les seigneurs qui soufflent
    sur la poussière pour irriter les âmes d'eau et de feu et
    leur suite suant l'angoisse
Les maîtres d'en haut riant à fleurs écloses et d'en bas
    plus éteints qu'un foyer asphyxié par leur haleine ne
    recevront jamais assez de coeurs conquis de haute lutte
    sur un partenaire exalté par un amour solaire
Il y a de quoi Le héros tout mouillé franchit d'un bond
    lumineux une étendue battant des mains neigeuses à
    son passage et tous le saluent d'une goutte ou d'un lac
    de vie jusqu'à ce qu'il retourne sommeiller sur sa couche
    de plumes d'aigles abattus
Mais voici qu'il entraîne dans son sillage de maïs en fleur
    des silhouettes vaporeuses de visages blancs à barbe de
    caverne abritant mille scorpions au dard dressé et des
    rumeurs impalpables de centaures s'ebrouant dans des
    hennissements issus d'un sol révolté
Nul doute que le grand serpent à plumes las d'une migration
    sans espoir ne revienne vers son peuple aux yeux de
    cratère les mains pleines de fleurs à chants de cristal
    arrachés à la nuit et de fruits qui dorent la vie cueillis
    entre les deux étoiles qui jalonnent le sentier où du
    souvenir de Tollan sanctifié par des vagabondages guidés
    par des aigles et des jaguars l'avait chassé la fourberie
    d'un miroir fumant
Non pourtant l'abjecte croix qui supprime lance des feux
    de supplice et l'hostie variolée pourrit celui qu'elle
    touche
Ils vont rejetant de loin les hommes chez leurs ancêtres
    sans que les précède aucun chien rouge pour les
    conduire par les déserts sans jour et sans nuit les froids
    qui font s'éparpiller l'âme et les torrents insultants que
    nul ne peut asservir
Précédés d'hommes aux paroles de péché vêtus de robes
    de boue grasse et qui *balaient les plats avec leur nez*
    tous ils exigent l'or qui ne vaut pas les plumes du matin
    et du soir et torturent au nom d'un monarque agenouillé
    devant deux baguettes entrecroisées

Printemps plus jamais tu ne seras écorché
et toi maïs vert plus jamais tu ne seras honoré

Here in their blood-haloed haunts will live the true Aztec chiefs
of day and night lords who blow on dust to arouse water spirits
fire spirits and their anguish-racked suite
The masters on high laughing like full-blown flowers and below
more dead than a hearth asphyxiated by their breath will
never have their fill of hearts won in full battle from an
opponent impassioned with solar love
There's a good reason The still-damp hero leaps brightly over
an expanse clapping snowy hands as he passes and all greet
him with a drop of water or with a lake of life until he
returns to sleep on his bed of slain eagle's feathers
But behold he bears off in his wake of flowering corn vaporous
forms with white faces and cave beards hiding a thousand
scorpions with their stings raised and the imperceptible
clamor of whinnying centaurs that come from a rebel earth
No doubt that the great plumed serpent weary from hopeless migration
will return to its people crater-eyed hands full of crystal
song-flowers plucked from the night full of fruits gilding
their lives fruits picked between the two stars that mark
the path along which a smoking mirror's deceit had chased
it away from the memory of Tollan* hallowed by wanderings
guided by eagles and jaguars
Oh no the abject cross that kills casts torture fires and the
host marked by smallpox decays all it touches
They go on casting men far off their ancestors' home without a
single red dog in front to guide them over deserts devoid
of night and day through chill winds that fracture the soul
and insulting untamed floods
Led by men with sinful words dressed in robes of thick mud
sweeping dishes with their noses all demand gold valueless
when weighed against the feathers of morning or night and
commit tortures in the name of a king kneeling before
two crossed rods**

Springtime never more will you be flayed
and you green corn never again will you be honored

* Tollan, a city, the modern Tula in the Valley of Tula in Hidalgo.

** According to the Mayan Bible, *Popol Vuh*, there exists a cross indicating the four cardinal
points. This image was ultimately assimilated with the image of the Christian cross.

D'un crucifix sanglant les *mangeurs d'anones portant un*
cercle sur la tête veulent faire *un dieu qui n'est pas*
nécessaire puisque tous vivent parmi les hommes
Ils détruisent pour lui les demeures des maîtres du vent et
du feu et de tout ce qui vit et meurt et les livres de toute
science
La nuit haletante de désir n'a pas connu six fois de suite
l'hommage rajeunissant d'une flamme brisant sa coquille
et ne brûlant que pour le serpent de lait et les siens
Les étrangers n'ont allumé que des bûchers pour ceux
que le soleil enchante de vols pouffant de rire qui
saluent la grenouille s'épuisant à les nourrir et craignent
que ne s'éveille le géant qui ronfle sous les montagnes
l'abritant des grands vents qui balaient la terre pour que
Tlaloc s'y repose
Qu'ils rentrent chevauchant des mâchoires multipliées au
fond des vagues où le soleil se frotte les yeux les blancs
à pelage d'hostie qui avec l'eau ont fait entrer dans les
têtes la taupe de la faim et le fouet du patron nourri
d'Indiens morts
et de la femme blanche qui s'étonne de se voir dans un lac
comme des vallées formées en s'asseyant par les
seigneurs de la terre ou du ciel de chaque épi et de
chaque langue s'enfle un air de liberté plus brûlant que
celui des déserts calcinés par le tyran de l'été pour que
l'étranger y aiguise un appétit de vautour
Un chant qui arrache les anneaux aux esclaves étonnés de
respirer la lumière emporte la galère comme un boeuf
noyé et chassant la tourbe obscure des lécheurs de
crucifix attise l'ardeur du feu qui reconnaît ses créatures
L'air sera plus clair si n'y retentissent que des voix sans
espion ni contrainte
L'eau sera plus limpide si ne s'y reflètent que des visages
sans angoisse ne péché
La neige des pics griffant les nuages sera plus éclatante de
n'être foulée que par des pas sans entrave
Les chemins ne mèneront plus au silence des tombeaux
affamés mais aux jeux des oiseaux pleuvant du soleil
Les sources ne chanteront plus jamais de complaintes
d'éternels condamnés mais riront de toutes leurs dents
de printemps

From a bloody crucifix the *prayer mumblers wearing*
   circles on their heads want to create a god *who is*
   unnecessary since all live in the world of men
For him they destroy the abodes of the masters of wind and
   fire and of all things that live and die and the books of
   every science
Night panting with desire has not seen six times over
   the youth-bestowing homage of a flame bursting its shell
   and burning only for the milk snake and its followers
The foreigners lit only funeral pyres for those whom the sun
   charms with flights swelled with laughter which greet the
   frog straining to feed them and fear that the giant might
   be roused the giant snoring under the mountains sheltering him
   from the great winds that swept the earth so that Tlaloc
   might rest
Let them return riding jaws profuse beneath the waves where the
   sun rubs its eyes the whites with fur of eucharistic hosts
   which have drummed into people's heads with water the mole
   of hunger and the whip of bosses fattened on dead Indians
and from the white woman surprised to see herself in a lake
   shaped like valleys while sitting by the lords of heaven
   and earth from each ear of corn and from each tongue mounts
   a song of liberty hotter than that of deserts baked by the
   tyrant of summer so that the foreigner may sharpen his
   vulture's appetite
A song that breaks the shackles of slaves amazed that they now
   breathe light bears off the galley like a drowned ox and
   driving out the dark mob of crucifix-lickers kindles the
   heat of the fire that claims its own creatures
The air will be clearer filled only with voices void
   of spies or constraints
The water will be more limpid reflecting only faces
   free from suffering and sin
The snow of peak-scraping clouds will be brighter
   trod only by unfettered steps
Roads will no longer lead to the silence of famished tombs
   but to the sport of birds raining from the sun
Springs will never more sing laments of men condemned for
   life but will laugh with all their springtime teeth

Le maïs s'élancera plus haut de n'avoir pas à courber la tête
    comme un christ ployant sous la charge
Même l'or sera plus pur de ne parer que des sourires à
    affoler les nuits balayées de chaudes brises étoilées de
    baisers
Hélas ceux qui hument du porridge écoutent dans les
    montagnes qui dissimulent le sommeil de l'or d'en haut
    tinter celui d'en bas
L'étranger à face d'éponge repue a prouvé aux hommes
    qu'un reflet de lumière vénéneuse peut massacrer pour
    peupler d'esclaves les vies éternelles des manieurs de
    croix
et quelqu'un la main en mare sans feux-follets malgré les
    fermentations inépuisables qui crèvent à sa surface leur
    ouvre les portes aux poignards entre deux épaules
De la tête arrachée comme d'un arbre emporté par une
    tornade à maîtriser d'une camisole de force vont
    s'échapper vers le Nord stérilisant les joyaux secrets
    jalousement gardés par les génies opaques des ténèbres
    pesantes et les fruits sans cesse renouvelés d'une union
    qui appelle des torrents de larmes d'allégresse
et le corps déchiré de rages de taureau défié mais qui veut
    retrouver un jour délivré des brouillards aux ventouses
    suspectes attend que Juares l'épouille et disperse les
    vols noirs dégoulinant de latin
Rien n'y fait L'homme qui vit du soleil battant la charge
    est devenu un champion de cave pour les rats de la terre
    et la terre meurt de faim tandis qu'un crapaud enfle
    jusqu'à se croire général de ses pustules
Mais une voix d'alouette éblouie s'élève du sol baillonné
    pour exiger que les portes aux verrous de fusillades
    soient ouvertes comme la mer à l'horizon qui s'allume
    pour une fête d'égaux
Parti du coeur broyé par une angoisse sans aube imaginable
    elle s'éloigne en avalanche qui fait palpiter jusqu'aux
    veines du marbre et rebondit en tonnerre remplissant les
    vallées soudain étonnées que leur paix soit celle des os
    décapés
Les forêts de têtes penchées se redressent et s'illuminent de
    regards qui explosent en justice sommaire et toutes les
    huttes de misère séchée abritent un être qui se condense
    en homme

Corn will shoot up higher no longer having to bow its head
        like a burdened christ
Even gold will be purer now only adorning smiles made to
        craze nights swept with warm breezes starred with kisses
Alas those who sniff porridge hear in concealing mountains
        the sleep of gold from on high ring its counterpart below
The stranger with the face of sated sponge has proved to men
        that a beam of poisonous light can kill in order to people
        with slaves the eternal lives of cross-wielders
and someone his hand in a pond without will-o'-the-wisps despite
        endless fermentation bubbling to the surface opens the
        doors to daggers between two shoulders
From the head torn off like a tree swept away by a
        tornado controlled only by a straitjacket secret joys
        will escape to the sterilizing North secret joys jealously
        guarded by the opaque spirits of ponderous darkness and
        by the fruits ceaselessly renewed of a union evoking floods
        of joyful tears
and the body racked with the rage of a challenged bull but which
        wants to rediscover a day delivered from nights with suspicious
        suckers waits for Juarez to cleanse it and to disperse the
        black flights dripping latin
Nothing can be done The man who lives on sun sounding the battle
        charge has become a cave champion for the rats of the earth
        and the earth is dying of hunger while a toad puffs up and
        considers himself general of his pimples
But the voice like a dazzled swallow rises from the gagged ground
        to demand that the gates with bolts of rifle-fire be opened
        like the sea near the horizon which lights up to celebrate
        equality
Taking flight from a heart worn with anguish void of foreseeable
        dawn the voice strikes out in an avalanche that makes even
        marble veins tremble and resounds in thunder filling the
        valleys suddenly amazed that their peace should be a peace
        of bleached bones
Forests of heads stand up and shine out with looks exploding
        in summary justice and all the sacks of dried-up misery
        shelter a being that condenses into man

La vie ne peut plus être une reptation bénie des providences
   complices du sillon de chiourme assommée au squelette
   privé de revenant puisque de chaque sillon pareil à un
   sou neuf Zapata fait lever la moisson à jamais mûre des
   chants déshérités

Hélas rien qu'un épars Demain la foudre
Les Voilà qui reviennent les ombres barbares à face de dollar
   numéroté Regardez-les ronger les pierres qui portent la
   honte au front ronger la terre les voudrait dissoudre
   ronger les hommes jusqu'au coeur qu'elles empestent

Paris, Septembre 1949.

Life can no longer be grovelling blessed by heavenly powers
in collusion with a furrow like a convict beaten to the
bones deprived of a ghost since each furrow like a new
Zapata penny gives rise to the ever-ripe harvest of songs
of the disinherited

Alas nothing but a scattered Tomorrow the lightning bolt
There They are returning from barbaric shadows with faces of
numbered dollar bills See them gnaw the stones that bring
shame gnaw the earth that feels like dissolving them gnaw
the hearts of men whom they foul

Paris, September 1949

❦ AUTRES POÈMES

Le Boeuf . . .

Le boeuf à fermeture éclair
ressemble à ton grand-père
à mon grand-père
à celui de tous
bien que ses moustaches aient un air d'adverbe
que ses yeux pleurent comme un escalier où manque une
    marche
et supplient les vols d'hirondelles
de lui accorder un chapeau de curé
à fermeture éclair
Mais le chapeau de curé
frémit tout au long de sa fermeture éclair
frontière dont chaque dent cache un douanier
gueule de crocodile guignant une jambe
et cherche un curé vide
à fermeture éclair
à soutane mouchetée d'hosties où fermentent des Verboten
éclatant comme des vesses-de-loup
qui projettent des psaumes poussiéreux et las
à l'image d'un oeillet d'Inde fané
ou d'une concierge
à fermeture e'clair
comme son Dites votre nom après dix heures
où transparaît une scie ébréchée
pleine de rancoeur
et décidée à se venger

❧ OTHER POEMS

The Steer . . .

The steer with a zipper
looks like your grandfather
my grandfather
everybody's grandfather
even though its mustache looks like an adverb
and its eyes weep like stairs with a step missing
they plead flights of swallows
to grant him a priest's hat
with a zipper
But the priest's hat
shudders all along its zipper
a frontier where each tooth hides a customs officer
a crocodile's jaws ogling a leg
and looks for an empty priest
with a zipper
with a cassock spotted with hosts in which Verbotens ferment
bursting like puffballs
which throw tired and dusty psalms
at the picture of a faded Indian carnation
or of a concierge
with a zipper
like her Tell me your name after ten o'clock*
where a broken saw shows through
full of rancor
and bent on revenge

* After ten o'clock, when the doors of French apartment buildings are locked, the concierge insists that anyone wishing to enter give his or her name.

sur un passant bigle comme un meuble rongé par les vers
sourd comme une cervelle aplatie par le temps
et muet comme une brique
à fermeture éclair

Dernièrement

À mi-chemin entre le promontoire armé jusqu'aux dents
et la rivière qui fait des grâces
s'avance la grosse bête dont chaque poil est un oeil
tantôt ouvert
tantôt fermé
au regard plus franc qu'un sou neuf
ou sournois comme un dé à coudre
qui se dirige vers la mer toute tremblante
du pas lourd de mille tombereaux qu'on ne déchargera jamais
ou d'un banc d'huîtres qui digèrent
Et la bête plus longue que la nuit précédant l'élargissement
        du condamné
plus massive qu'un tonneau de choucroute en fermentation
pénètre dans la mer qui recule
comme une locomotive manoeuvrant à la recherche de ses
        wagons
Jusqu'où devra-t-elle reculer
Jusqu'à l'automne l'automne prochain où les chiens perdront
        leur peau
qui tournoiera dans les nuages de fonte comme un épervier
        en chasse
puis ira vêtir des pierres humides qui feront le gros dos
ou bien jusqu'à la rue déserte
où l'on ne voit que des dentelles de maisons

against a passerby as cockeyed as a worm-eaten piece of furniture
as deaf as brains beaten down by time
as dumb as a brick
with a zipper

Lately

Halfway between the promontory armed to the teeth
and the river that puts on airs
comes the great beast
each of his hairs is an eye
sometimes open
sometimes closed
with an expression more frank than a new penny
or crafty as a thimble
that goes toward the ocean trembling all over
with the heavy gait of a thousand wheelbarrows that will never be emptied
or of an oyster bed that is digesting
And that beast longer than the night preceding the release of
    a convict
more massive than a barrel of fermenting sauerkraut
dives into the ocean which pulls back
like a locomotive maneuvering to find its cars
How far will it pull back
Until autumn next autumn when dogs will shed their skins
which will swirl in clouds of slush like a sparrow hawk
    in pursuit
then will go off to clothe wet stones which will arch up
or else it will pull back to the deserted street
where you can only see the lacework of houses

APPENDIX
PÉRET'S WORKS: A PERSPECTIVE

Consistent is the best word to describe the forty-year span of Benjamin Péret's poetry. Discovering immediately a poetic style and a poetic idiom that reflected an authentic personality and exemplified the Surrealist aims of freedom and creativity, throughout his lifetime he wrote and published a trajectory of poems. Their subjects might vary, the focus change, the emotions alter, but an essential style and quality always rang true to the initial conception. One cannot exactly speak of development throughout the years, only of gentle evolution.

His first collection, *Le Passager du transatlantique*, appeared in 1921 in the burgeoning stages of the Surrealist movement, when the spirits of Dada and Surrealism together challenged existing literary traditions. "En avant" is the first of eleven poems and irresistibly communicates the spirit of enthusiastic adventure characterizing them all. The theme of ocean voyage appears in all the titles. Sometimes this carries through in the verse, sometimes not. Yet the sense of break with tradition, of play, of good-natured direct humor is very contagious. "Babord pour tous" suggests a play on words, "babord-d'abord," which in the translation is meta-morphosed into "port-but." This play is reinforced in the serial structure and ends with a free sense of motion, with an irreverent exchange of insults between the passengers and the swallows. The third poem, "Passagers de seconde classe et leurs cheveux"—of which the unrelated title is nearly as long as the text—is simply a condensed, breathless, tit-for-tat about a happy, aimless trip.

The next publications are very different in subject and atmosphere. *Immortelle maladie* (1924) contains six medium-length poems, and *Dormir dormir dans les pierres* (1927) contains five longer ones. They are all serious, relating strange adventures in dreamlike, often apocalyptic settings. Some-times, as in "Soleil route usée . . . ," the role of the narrator, who is himself fascinated, is to relate extraordinary and often frightening occurrences and to comment or even command the peculiar turn of events. Sometimes, as in "Nue nue comme ma maîtresse," the narrator and his mistress appear in the story, the core of their beings borne up and borne off in the course of universal time with moments of pleasure and moments of anguish. These two collections have the flavor of a Jungian imagination. Since the Surrealists knew Freud's work and were directly influenced by it, and since some of Jung's writings had then been translated into French, it is not impossible that Péret was familiar with Jung's ideas as well as with Freud's. In any case, the archetypal imagery in these collections is rich, integrating the structure and pervading the deep preoccupations of the protagonists.

Le Grand jeu (1928) is the most extensive collection, with 110 poems. It is Péret's best-known book, perhaps since it appeared during the most active, creative years of the Surrealist movement, before the tensions and rivalries had surfaced. Certainly, Péret's poems at this stage of his life have a very special flair, verve, uninhibited humor, and an apparently inexhaustible wealth of invention. Most of them are fairly short, and the lines have a brisk, quick, easy rhythm. Many are gratuitously playful. Some touch on subjects close to Péret's social concerns, such as the anticlerical poem "Le langage des saints." The tone, if irreverent, is rarely acerbic.

My selection from this collection is intended to show the wide variety of its subjects. A few poems deserve special comment. "Portrait de Paul Éluard" is one of a number addressed to his friends. It is mainly light in tone, almost too familiarly absurd, but it reveals underneath a warm, serious current of friendship and of common interest and goals. "Le Mariage des feuilles" is one of the few poems in which Péret touches on the nature of poetry. He compares poetic rhythm to that of natural phenomena, botanical currents with a circular pattern of ebb and flow. In the first verse, the idea is presented directly; in the third verse, it is described using the images of dust and dancing slippers that restlessly, lightly move, turn, and dive. Another, "La Boîte aux lumières," suggests the fanciful volatility of the Surrealist imagination. From the box full of light cotton, subject to whims at the least change of weather or sentiment, the poem moves through several strange visions that include spinach and mice in a world of delights. The final poem of the collection, "Le Quart d'une vie," is very different, resembling in form a medieval "testament." It has sixteen short parts, each describing a scene in a strange world where the narrator is a spectator to events, both unusual and ordinary, interspersed with commonplace comments: "So be it." But the final part expresses weariness: "My pipe is dead / and my wide eye is dreary." This poem suggests oddly juxtaposed echoes of François Villon and of the Arthur Rimbaud in "Après le déluge." It is, I believe, basically serious.

In the Losfeld edition of Péret's works, the next volume represented is

Je ne mange pas de ce pain-là (1936), which includes twenty-eight poems entirely devoted to political attacks, virulent, generally crude, and comprehensive. They were written in the late twenties (after 1926) and in the early thirties. Some of them have a contemporary basis, such as the "conversion" of André Gide to communism, a eucharistic congress in Chicago, the League of Nations, the anonymous personalities of World War I veterans, distinct political personalities such as Aristide Briand and Raymond Poincaré, and riots such as the one connected with the Stavisky affair in February, 1934. Others conjure from the French past figures such as Jeanne d'Arc, Louis XVI, and Napoleon. They are merciless yet tempered with Péret's genuine conviction and with his typical down-to-earth imagery and casts of characters, including, for instance, the macaroni stuck in Poincaré's beard. His Trotskyite ideology was nurtured in the French tradition, heart-based, heartfelt, and expressed not only in words but also in action, for which he paid a price.

De Derrière les fagots (1934) is the second most extensive collection, containing sixty poems of remarkably consistent quality. They tend to be longer than those of *Le Grand jeu* and in a sense represent an amalgam of the willful playfulness characterizing *Immortelle maladie* and *Dormir dormir dans les pierres*. Many have as titles commonplace sayings or platitudes—for instance, "Quatre à quatre" and "Faire des pieds et des mains"—which serve as a familiar base for incursions into unfamiliar territories, complete with adventure, danger and rescue, challenge and laudable effort, a sense of the vulnerability of existence and of the possibility of hope even in seemingly desperate situations. "Mille fois" is typical in this respect, starting with the suggestion that when you find a chocolate bar in the gilded ruins of a gas factory, a chase will ensue leading you far and wide. You'll meet a train that doesn't stop at a little station, for a number of good reasons, and you'll become aware of several unusual possibilities that, if they come to pass, will usher forth a new and better world where the gentle and the good triumph. All of these poems in a sense call into question everything we take for granted. They recall Henri Michaux's innocent abroad in *Au Pays de la magie*—another twentieth-century counterpart of Montesquieu with a concern for justice, social customs, and relationships—as they present questions about causality, about expectations, hopeful or disquieting, and also, as in the case of poems such as "Chasse à courre" and "Qui est-ce," fundamental questions about identity and the formation and deformation of reality by words.

There is one short but very sweet volume of love poems, *Je Sublime*, containing sixteen poems written between January and March, 1935, and published in 1936. They are addressed to "Rosa." Many touch directly on communication, such as "Allo" and "Parle-moi," where the sound of her voice, her glances, and the interior echoes of her name nurture an invasive, manifold presence, occupying his thoughts and pervading his very being. The most beautiful of these, I find, is "Source," combining the fresh image of cool white wine, the erotic image of a wild bull from the waterfall, and the physical imagery of eating, drinking, and sleeping with Rosa finally deified in a dreamlike vision at daybreak.

After this, there was a period of nearly ten years when Péret's creative concerns were to some extent interrupted by the appeals, demands, and effects of world events in the context of his life: the Spanish Civil War in 1936, World War II beginning in 1940, exile in Mexico during the following years. In 1947, he published a collective edition, *Feu central*, which included the earlier works *Immortelle maladie*, *Dormir dormir dans les pierres*, and *Je Sublime*, and two new groups of poems, *Un Point c'est tout* and *À Tâtons*. He selected for *Feu central*, I presume, what he considered the best of his works to date. It is the one volume that most broadly represents his finest work. *Un Point c'est tout*, a collection of eleven poems first published in 1946, contains several love poems. These sometimes have an undercurrent of anxiety, such as "Un Matin," a dreamlike sequence depicting fears of loss. *À Tâtons*, a group of ten poems, appeared for the first time in *Feu central*. Some of these also are flecked with troubled thoughts, but they preserve Péret's infallible, playful, warm narrative style, as in "Le Premier Jour," a dream of which the cast is an apparently newly invented alphabet, and some have a mature, reflective cast, for example, "Reçu."

The inclusion of *Immortelle maladie* and *Dormir dormir dans les pierres* in the collective edition is interesting because it suggests that Péret considered his archetypal poetry to represent a very important facet of his creative imagination. Especially so, since two other major poems from this later period are similar in inspiration, more lengthy, nearly of epic proportions. The first of these is *Dernier malheur dernière chance*, written in Mexico in 1942, a twenty-five page narrative relating the cataclysmic birth, evolution, and the violent yet lovely and delicate fruition of the earth and of earthly forces and beings. This poem is nonspecific, in contrast to *Air mexicain*, which was inspired by the years he lived in Mexico, close in spirit to the land, to its people, and to its past. *Air mexicain* was written in 1949, soon after his return to Paris. It relates Mexico's legends and history, the succession of gods and violent forces of life and death from an original creator, through the Mayan deities, through the Christian gods imposed by the Spaniards, through the national hero Zapata, to the god dollar of the twentieth century. Of all his poems, it is the least easily accessible, because of the density and multiplicity of the imagery and because of the length and sustained energy of the rhetorical periods. Yet I believe it is his ultimate creation, a fine fresco that melds the judgment and sophistication of a modern man's insights with an empathized primitive imagination—in his own view, the most valuable and the purest expression of the human spirit.

However, the demands of epic invention are too great for one human being to sustain for long. Péret's last poems return to the humor and to the intimate mortal insights of his earlier years. "Dernièrement," the last poem chosen for this selection, reveals the beast of time and a final image, the lacework of houses along a deserted street.